Disney · PIXAR

엘리멘탈

CONTENTS

ABOUT ELEMENTAL · 4
이 책의 구성 · 6
이 책의 활용법 · 8

PROLOGUE
● Quiz & Words List ·· 10

CHAPTERS 1 & 2
● Quiz & Words List ·· 26

CHAPTERS 3 & 4
● Quiz & Words List ·· 42

CHAPTERS 5 & 6
● Quiz & Words List ·· 64

CHAPTERS 7 & 8
● Quiz & Words List ·· 84

CHAPTERS 9 & 10
● Quiz & Words List ·· 102

CHAPTERS 11 & 12
● Quiz & Words List ·· 122

CHAPTERS 13 & 14

● Quiz & Words List ·· 138

CHAPTERS 15 & 16

● Quiz & Words List ·· 162

CHAPTERS 17 & 18

● Quiz & Words List ·· 182

영어원서 읽기 TIPS · 202
ANSWER KEY · 208

QR코드를 스마트폰으로 인식하여 『ELEMENTAL』
오디오북과 한국어 번역 파일을 확인해 보세요!

**불, 물, 공기, 흙 4개의 원소들이 공존하는 신비의 세계,
'엘리먼트 시티'에 오신 것을 환영합니다!**

고향인 파이어 랜드에서 엘리멘탈 시티로 이주해 온 불의 원소 버니와 신더는 파이어플레이스라는 가게를 운영해 오고 있습니다. 두 사람의 딸인 앰버의 꿈은 부모님이 오랫동안 꾸려 온 이 가게를 물려받는 것입니다. 어느 날, 앰버는 가게에 밀려오는 손님들의 지나친 요구에 화를 참지 못해 결국 폭발하고, 그로 인해 가게 지하실의 수도관이 터지고 맙니다. 이때 터진 수도관을 통해 물의 원소 웨이드가 갑자기 가게로 흘러 들어오게 됩니다. 시청 공무원인 웨이드는 가게에 엄청나게 많은 위반 딱지를 발급하여 가게는 폐업 위기에 처하게 됩니다. 그러나 앰버의 자초지종을 듣고 감동한 웨이드는 가게의 폐업을 막기로 결심하고, 앰버와 함께 자신의 상사 게일을 찾아갑니다. 게일은 앰버에게 오래전 물이 끊긴 파이어타운에 물이 새는 근본적인 원인을 찾아 해결하면, 가게의 폐업을 없던 일로 해 주겠다고 약속합니다.

누수의 원인을 함께 찾아 나가는 과정에서 앰버와 웨이드는 서로에게 강한 사랑의 감정을 느끼게 됩니다. 원소끼리는 서로 섞일 수 없다는 말을 들으며 자라 온 앰버는 어떻게든 자신의 감정을 떨쳐내려 하지만, 그때마다 웨이드는 더욱 적극적으로 자신의 감정을 표현하죠. 부서진 수문이 누수의 원인이라는 것을 알게 된 앰버는 자신의 불을 이용해 모래로 유리를 만들어 수문을 막는 데 성공합니다. 웨이드의 가족은 앰버의 예술적 재능을 알아보고 그녀에게 유리 회사 인턴직을 제안하지만, 앰버는 부모님의 희생에 보답하는 길은 가게를 물려받는 것뿐이라며 결국 웨이드를 떠나고 맙니다.

바로 그때, 앰버가 유리로 막아 놓은 수문에 다시 금이 가기 시작하더니, 결국 엄청난 양의 물이 파이어 타운을 향해 쏟아져 나오기 시작합니다. 앰버와 웨이드는 서로를 받아들이고 함께 마을을 구할 수 있을까요? 앰버는 자신이 진정으로 하고 싶은 꿈을 찾는 용기를 낼 수 있을까요? 서로 반대라서 더 끌리는 열정적인 앰버와 감성적인 웨이드의 특별한 여정을 그려 낸 〈엘리멘탈〉을 지금 영화로 읽는 영어원서를 통해 읽어 보세요!

한국인을 위한 맞춤형 영어원서!

원서 읽기는 모두가 인정하는 최고의 영어 공부법입니다. 하지만 영어 구사력이 뛰어나지 않은 보통 영어 학습자들에게는 원서 읽기를 선뜻 시작하기가 부담되는 것도 사실입니다.

이 책은 영어 초보자들도 쉽게 원서 읽기를 시작하고, 꾸준한 읽기를 통해 '영어 원서 읽기 습관'을 형성할 수 있도록 만들어진 책입니다. 남녀노소 누구나 좋아할 만한 내용의 원서를 기반으로 내용 이해와 영어 실력 향상을 위한 다양한 콘텐츠를 덧붙이고, 리스닝과 낭독 훈련에 활용할 수 있는 오디오북까지 함께 제공하여, 원서를 부담 없이 읽으면서 자연스럽게 영어 실력을 향상시킬 수 있도록 도와줍니다.

특히 이 책은 원서와 워크북을 분권하여 휴대와 학습이 효과적으로 이루어지도록 배려했습니다. 이는 일반 원서에서 찾아볼 수 없는 특장점으로, 워크북과 오디오북을 적절히 활용하면 더욱 쉽고 재미있게 영어 실력을 향상시킬 수 있습니다. ('원서'와 '워크북' 및 '오디오북 MP3 파일' 3종으로 구성된 패키지가 이상 없이 갖추어져 있는지 다시 한번 확인해 보세요!)

이런 분들께 강력 추천합니다!

- 영어원서 읽기를 처음 시작하는 독자
- 쉽고 재미있는 원서를 찾고 있는 영어 학습자
- 영화 『엘리멘탈』을 재미있게 보신 분
- 특목고 입시를 준비하는 초·중학생
- 토익 600~750점, 고등학교 상위권 수준의 영어 학습자

이 책의 구성

본문 텍스트

내용이 담긴 본문입니다.
원어민이 읽는 일반 원서와 같은 텍스트지만, 암기해야 할 중요 어휘들은 볼드체로 표시되어 있습니다. 이 어휘들은 지금 들고 계신 워크북에 챕터별로 정리되어 있습니다.

학습 심리학 연구 결과에 따르면, 한 단어씩 따로 외우는 단어 암기는 거의 효과가 없다고 합니다. 단어를 제대로 외우기 위해서는 문맥(context) 속에서 단어를 암기해야 하며, 한 단어당 문맥 속에서 15번 이상 마주칠 때 완벽하게 암기할 수 있다고 합니다.

이 책의 본문에서는 중요 어휘를 볼드체로 강조하여, 문맥 속의 단어들을 더 확실히 인지(word cognition in context)하도록 돕고 있습니다. 또한 대부분의 중요 단어들은 다른 챕터에서도 반복해서 등장하기 때문에 이 책을 읽는 것만으로도 자연스럽게 어휘력을 향상시킬 수 있습니다.

또한 본문 하단에는 내용 이해를 돕기 위한 '각주'가 첨가되어 있습니다. 각주는 굳이 암기할 필요는 없지만, 알아 두면 도움이 될 만한 정보를 설명하고 있습니다. 각주를 참고하면 스토리를 더 깊이 있게 이해할 수 있어 원서를 읽는 재미가 배가됩니다.

워크북(Workbook)

Check Your Reading Speed

챕터마다 단어 수가 기록되어 있어, 리딩 속도를 측정할 수 있습니다. 특히 리딩 속도를 중시하는 독자들이 유용하게 사용할 수 있습니다.

Build Your Vocabulary

본문에 볼드 표시되어 있는 단어들이 정리되어 있습니다. 리딩 전·후에 반복해서 보면 원서를 더욱 쉽게 읽을 수 있고, 어휘력도 빠르게 향상될 것입니다.

단어는 〈빈도 – 스펠링 – 발음기호 – 품사 – 한글 뜻 – 영문 뜻〉 순서로 표기되어 있습니다. 품사는 아래와 같이 표기했습니다.

n. 명사 │ a. 형용사 │ ad. 부사 │ v. 동사
conj. 접속사 │ prep. 전치사 │ int. 감탄사 │ idiom 숙어 및 관용구

Comprehension Quiz

간단한 퀴즈를 통해 읽은 내용에 대한 이해력을 점검해 볼 수 있습니다.

영어원서 읽기, 이렇게 시작해 보세요!!

아래와 같이 프리뷰(Preview) → 리딩(Reading) → 리뷰(Review) 세 단계를 거치면서 원서를 읽으면, 더욱 효과적으로 영어 실력을 향상할 수 있습니다.

1. 프리뷰(Preview): 오늘 읽을 내용을 먼저 점검하자!

- 워크북을 통해 오늘 읽을 챕터에 나와 있는 단어들을 쭉 훑어봅니다. 어떤 단어들이 나오는지, 내가 아는 단어와 모르는 단어가 어떤 것들이 있는지 가벼운 마음으로 살펴봅니다.

- 평소처럼 하나하나 쓰면서 암기하려고 하지는 마세요! 익숙하지 않은 단어들을 주의 깊게 보되, 어차피 리딩을 하면서 점차 익숙해질 단어라는 것을 기억하며 빠르게 훑어봅니다.

- 뒤 챕터로 갈수록 반복해서 등장하는 단어들이 있다는 것을 알 수 있습니다. 매일매일 꾸준히 읽는다면, 눈에 익숙한 단어들이 점점 많아지고, 자연스럽게 암기되는 것을 몸으로 느낄 수 있습니다.

2. 리딩(Reading): 내용에 집중하며 빠르게 읽어 나가자!

- 프리뷰를 마친 후 바로 리딩을 시작합니다. 방금 살펴봤던 어휘들을 문장 속에서 다시 만나게 되는데, 이 과정에서 단어의 쓰임새와 어감을 자연스럽게 익히게 됩니다.

- 모르는 단어나 이해되지 않는 문장이 나오더라도 멈추지 말고 전체적인 맥락을 파악하면서 속도감 있게 읽어 나가세요. 이해되지 않는 문장들은 따로 표시를 하되, 일단 넘어가서 계속 읽는 것이 좋습니다. 뒷부분을 읽다 보면 자연히 이해가 되는 경우도 있고, 정 이해가 되지 않는 부분은 리딩을 마친 이후에 따로 리뷰하는 시간을 가지면 됩니다. 문제집을 풀듯이 모든 문장을 분석하면서 원서를 읽는 것이 아니라, 리딩할 때는 리딩에만, 리뷰할 때는 리뷰에만 집중하는 것이 필요합니다.

- 볼드 처리된 단어의 의미가 궁금하더라도, 워크북을 바로 펼치지 마세요. 정 궁금하다면 한 번씩 참고하는 것도 나쁘진 않지만, 워크북과 원서를 번갈아 보면서 읽는 것은 리딩의 흐름을 끊고 단어 하나하나에 집착하는 좋지 않은 리딩 습관을 심어 줄 수 있습니다.

- 같은 맥락에서 번역서를 구해 원서와 동시에 번갈아 보는 것도 좋은 방법이 아닙니다. 한글 번역을 가지고 있다고 해도 일단 영어로 읽을 때는 영어에만 집중하고 어느 정도 분량을 읽은 후에 번역서와 비교하도록 하세요. 처음부터 완벽하게 이해하려고 하는 것보다는 빠른 속도로 2-3회 반복해서 읽는 방식이 실력 향상에 더 도움이 됩니다. 만약 반복해서 읽어도 내용이 전혀 이해되지 않는다면 좀 더 쉬운 책을 골라 실력을 다진 뒤 다시 도전하는 것이 좋습니다.
- 초보자라면 분당 150단어의 리딩 속도를 목표로 잡고 리딩을 합니다. 분당 150단어는 원어민이 말하는 속도로, 영어 학습자들이 리스닝과 스피킹으로 넘어가기 위해 가장 기초적으로 달성해야 하는 단계입니다. 분당 50~80단어 정도의 낮은 리딩 속도를 가지고 있는 경우는 대부분 '잘못된 리딩 습관'을 가지고 있어서 그렇습니다. 이해력이 조금 떨어진다고 하더라도 분당 150단어까지는 속도감 있게 읽어 나가도록 하세요.

3. 리뷰(Review): 이해력을 점검하고 꼼꼼하게 다시 살펴보자!

- 해당 챕터의 Comprehension Quiz를 통해 이해력을 점검해 봅니다.
- 오늘 만난 어휘들을 다시 한번 복습합니다. 이때는 읽으면서 중요하다고 생각했던 단어를 연습장에 써 보면서 꼼꼼하게 외우는 것도 좋습니다.
- 이해가 되지 않는다고 표시해 두었던 부분도 주의 깊게 분석해 봅니다. 다시 한번 문장을 꼼꼼히 읽고, 어떤 이유에서 이해가 되지 않았는지 생각해 봅니다. 따로 메모를 남기거나 노트를 작성하는 것도 좋은 방법입니다.
- 원서를 읽고 리뷰하는 시간을 가지는 것은 영어 실력 향상에 많은 도움이 되기는 하지만, 이 과정을 철저히 지키려다가 원서 읽기의 재미를 반감시키는 것은 바람직하지 않습니다. 그럴 때는 차라리 리뷰를 가볍게 하는 것이 좋을 수 있습니다. '내용에 빠져서 재미있게', 문제집에서는 상상도 못할 '많은 양'을 읽으면서, 매일매일 조금씩 꾸준히 실력을 키워 가는 것이 원서를 활용하는 기본적인 방법이며, 영어 공부의 왕도입니다. 문제집 풀듯이 원서 읽기를 시도하고 접근해서는 실패할 수밖에 없습니다.
- 이런 방식으로 원서를 끝까지 다 읽었다면, 다시 반복해서 읽거나 오디오북을 활용하는 등 다양한 방식으로 원서 읽기를 확장해 나갈 수 있습니다. 이에 대한 자세한 안내가 워크북 말미에 실려 있습니다.

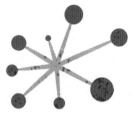

Prologue

1. What did the Blue Flame represent?

    A. The name of the boat they were on

    B. The symbol of city they were headed

    C. The traditions and heritage of Fire Land

    D. The personality of the baby they were expecting

2. What was Bernie's plan for their new home's first floor?

    A. To make it a playroom for the baby

    B. To turn it into a shop

    C. To turn it into a library

    D. To make it a kitchen

3. What did Bernie teach Ember about his homeland?

A. The language, values, and customs

B. How to cook traditional food

C. How to make traditional clothes

D. The details of important locations

4. What did Bernie tell Ember about the shop?

A. That its history is a secret

B. That it will all be hers someday

C. That it is too big for them

D. That they will sell it soon

5. How did Ember feel about taking over the shop?

A. Scared

B. Surprised

C. Uninterested

D. Determined

Check Your Reading Speed

1분에 몇 단어를 읽는지 리딩 속도를 측정해보세요.

$$\frac{1{,}478 \text{ words}}{\text{reading time ( ) sec}} \times 60 = (\quad) \text{ WPM}$$

Build Your Vocabulary

aboard [əbɔ́ːrd] prep. (배·기차·비행기 등에) 탄
If you are aboard a ship or plane, you are on it or in it.

flaming [fléimiŋ] a. 불타는
Flaming describes something that is burning or on fire.

outline [áutlain] n. 윤곽
The outline of something is its general shape, especially when it cannot be clearly seen.

illuminate [ilúːmənèit] v. 비추다
To illuminate something means to shine light on it and to make it brighter and more visible.

await [əwéit] v. 기다리다
If you await someone or something, you wait for them.

shore [ʃɔːr] n. 해안가
The shore is the land along the edge of a sea, lake, or wide river.

possession [pəzéʃən] n. 소지품
Your possessions are the things that you own or have with you at a particular time.

flame [fleim] n. 불꽃
A flame is the hot, bright, and burning gas produced by something on fire.

contain [kəntéin] v. 담다
To contain means to hold or have something within itself.

precious [préʃəs] a. 소중한
Something that is precious has great value or importance, often because it is rare or special.

represent [rèprizént] v. 상징하다
To represent is to be a symbol or example of something.

tradition [trədíʃən] n. 전통
A tradition is a custom or belief that has existed for a long time.

heritage [héritidʒ] n. 유산
Heritage is the history, culture, and traditions that a group of people or a country has.

gently [dʒéntli] ad. 부드럽게
Gently means in a kind, mild, or careful manner.

belly [béli] n. 배, 복부
The belly is the front part of a person's or animal's body, between the chest and legs.

anticipate [æntísəpèit] v. 기대하다
To anticipate is to expect or predict that something will happen.

lean [liːn] v. (몸을) 숙이다
When you lean in a particular direction, you bend your body in that direction.

head [hed] v. (특정 방향으로) 가다
If you are heading for a particular place, you are going toward that place.

into the distance idiom 저 멀리, 먼 곳에 (= in the distance)
If you can see something into the distance, you can see it, far away from you.

element [éləmənt] n. 원소
An element is one of the four substances (earth, air, fire, and water) from which people used to believe that everything was made.

skyscraper [skáiskrèipər] n. 고층 건물
A skyscraper is a very tall building, often found in cities.

top [tap] v. (다른 것의) 위에 놓다
If something is topped with something, it has that thing as its highest part.

waterway [wɔ́ːtərwèi] n. 수로
A waterway is a river, canal, or other route for travel by water.

balloon [bəlúːn] n. 열기구 풍선
A balloon is a large bag made of strong material that is filled with hot air or gas to make it rise in the air, usually carrying a basket for passengers.

blimp [blimp] n. 비행선
A blimp is a large aircraft without wings, filled with a gas that is lighter than air, and driven by engines.

citizen [sítəzən] n. 시민
A citizen is a person who lives in and belongs to a particular city, town, or country.

typical [típikəl] a. 보통의
Typical means happening in the usual way.

varying [vé:riŋ] a. 다양한, 각기 다른
Varying things are things that are different from each other in size, amount, or degree.

shade [ʃeid] n. 색조
A shade of a particular color is one of its different forms.

slosh [slaʃ] v. 철벅거리다
If a liquid sloshes around, it moves in a noisy or messy way.

sidewalk [sáidwɔːk] n. 보도
A sidewalk is a path with a hard surface by the side of a road.

earth [əːrθ] n. 흙
Earth is the substance in which plants grow that covers most of the land.

branch [brænʧ] n. 나뭇가지
A branch is a part of a tree that grows out from the trunk and on which leaves, flowers, and fruit grow.

drift [drift] v. 떠다니다
When something drifts somewhere, it is carried there by the movement of wind or water.

near [niər] v. 가까이 가다
When you near a place, you come closer to it.

shoreline [ʃɔ́ːrlàin] n. 해안선
The shoreline is the line where the land meets the sea or other large body of water.

baby-to-be [béibi-tə-biː] n. 곧 태어날 아기
A baby-to-be is an unborn child, often referred to when discussing the future arrival of a baby.

relieved [rilíːvd] a. 안도하는
If you are relieved, you feel happy because something unpleasant has not happended or you are not worried about something any more.

solid [sálid] a. 단단한
Solid means firm, strong, or not easily broken.

dock [dak] v. (배를) 부두에 대다
If a ship docks or you dock a ship, it sails into a harbor and stays there.

nearby [niərbái] ad. 인근에, 가까운 곳에
If something is nearby, it is only a short distance away.

leafy [líːfi] a. 잎이 많은
Leafy describes something that has many leaves or is covered with leaves.

sprout [spraut] v. 생기다, 나타나다; 싹트게 하다
If a large number of things have appeared or developed somewhere, you can say that they have sprouted there or that the place has sprouted them.

passenger [pǽsəndʒər] n. 승객
A passenger in a vehicle such as a bus, boat, or plane is a person who is traveling in it, but who is not driving it or working on it.

file [fail] v. 줄지어 나오다
When a group of people files somewhere, they walk one behind the other in a line.

submarine [sÀbməríːn] n. 잠수함
A submarine is a type of ship that can travel both above and below the surface of the sea.

emerge [imə́ːrdʒ] v. 나타나다
To emerge means to come out from somewhere and become possible to see.

puddle [pʌdl] n. 웅덩이
A puddle is a small pool of liquid, especially water, that has collected on the ground.

gather [gǽðər] v. 챙기다, 모으다
If you gather things, you collect them together so that you can use them.

luggage [lʌ́gidʒ] n. 짐, 수하물
Luggage refers to the bags and suitcases that contain a traveler's personal belongings.

briefcase [brí:fkeis] n. 서류 가방
A briefcase is a flat, rectangular case with a handle, used for carrying documents or papers.

land [lænd] v. 착륙하다, 내려앉다
If a plane, bird, or insect lands, it moves safely down onto the ground.

perch [pəːrtʃ] n. 높은 장소
A perch is a high place or position, especially one where you can sit and watch something.

gust [gʌst] n. 돌풍
A gust is a strong, brief rush of air.

shoot [ʃuːt] v. (shot-shot) 휙 움직이다
If someone or something shoots in a particular direction, they move in that direction quickly and suddenly.

portal [pɔːrtl] n. 입구
A portal is an entrance or doorway, especially a large and impressive one.

disembark [dìsembáːrk] v. (배·비행기에서) 내리다
When you disembark, it means you leave a ship, aircraft, or other vehicles after a journey.

deflate [difléit] v. (공기가 빠져) 오므라들다
When something such as a tire or balloon deflates, or when you deflate it, all the air comes out of it.

board [bɔːrd] v. 탑승하다
To board means to get into or onto a means of transportation such as an airplane, bus, or ship.

puff up idiom 부풀다, 불룩해지다
If something puffs up, it looks bigger, usually because it has air in it.

immigration hall [iməgréiʃən hɔːl] n. 출입국 관리소
An immigration hall is a place where arriving passengers show their passports and have their luggage checked by officials.

pause [pɔːz] v. 잠시 멈추다
If you pause while you are doing something, you stop for a short period and then continue.

admire [ædmáiər] v. 감탄하며 바라보다
If you admire someone or something, you look at them with pleasure.

mural [mjúərəl] n. 벽화
A mural is a picture painted on a wall.

depict [dipíkt] v. 그리다
To depict means to show or represent by a drawing, painting, or other art forms.

immigrant [ímigrənt] n. 입국자, 이민자
An immigrant is a person who comes to live permanently in a foreign country.

make one's way idiom 나아가다
When you make your way somewhere, you walk or travel there.

official [əfíʃəl] n. 직원
An official is a person who holds a position of authority in an organization.

sizzle [sizl] v. 지글지글하는 소리를 내다
If something such as hot oil or fat sizzles, it makes hissing sounds.

go with idiom ~을 선택하다
If you go with something, you choose or select something.

stamp [stæmp] v. ~에 도장을 찍다
If you stamp a mark or word on an object, you press the mark or word onto the object using a special tool.

document [dákjumənt] n. 서류
A document is a piece of paper with official information on it.

bustling [bʌ́sliŋ] a. 북적거리는
If a place is bustling, it means it is full of energetic and noisy activity.

gaze [geiz] v. 응시하다, 바라보다
To gaze at something or someone means to look steadily and intently, especially in admiration, surprise, or thought.

canal [kənǽl] n. 운하
A canal is a long, narrow stretch of water that has been made for boats to travel along or to bring water to a particular area.

waterfall [wɔ́:tərfɔ:l] n. 폭포
A waterfall is a place where water flows over the edge of a steep, high cliff in hills or mountains, and falls into a pool below.

infrastructure [infrəstrʌ́kʧər] n. 기반 시설
Infrastructure refers to the basic systems that a country or organization needs in order to work properly, for example roads, railways and banks.

log [lɔ:g] n. 통나무
A log is a piece of a thick branch or of the trunk of a tree that has been cut so that it can be used for fuel or for making things.

vendor [véndər] n. 상인
A vendor is someone who sells things from a small stall or cart.

glide [glaid] v. 미끄러지듯 가다
To glide means to move smoothly and quietly, as if without effort or resistance.

waterslide [wɔ́:tərslaid] n. 물 미끄럼틀
A waterslide is a slide with water running down it.

block [blak] n. 구역, 블록
A block in a town or city is an area of land with streets on all its sides, or the area or distance between such streets.

tiny [táini] a. 아주 작은
Tiny describes something that is very small in size or extent.

extinguish [ikstíŋgwiʃ] v. (불을) 끄다
If you extinguish a fire or a light, you stop it burning or shining.

douse [daus] v. (물을) 끼얹다
If you douse someone or something with a liquid, you throw a lot of that liquid over them.

distracted [distrǽktid] a. (정신이) 산만해진
When someone is distracted, it means they are unable to concentrate because their thoughts are not focused.

sight [sait] n. 광경
A sight is something that you see.

separate [sépərèit] v. 분리하다
If you separate people or things that are together, they move apart.

suitcase [sú:tkeis] n. 여행 가방
A suitcase is a portable case, usually rectangular, used for carrying clothes and personal items when traveling.

rejoin [ri:dʒɔ́in] v. 재결합하다
To rejoin means to put or join together again.

apologize [əpálədʒàiz] v. 사과하다
To apologize means to express regret for something wrong that one has done.

zoom [zu:m] v. 쌩 하고 가다
To zoom means to move swiftly and directly, often in the context of a vehicle or on a means of transportation.

elevated [éləvèitid] a. (주변이나 지면보다) 높은
If land or buildings are elevated, they are raised up higher than the surrounding area.

crowded [kráudid] a. 붐비는
If a place is crowded, it is full of people.

shrink back idiom 뒷걸음질치다
To shrink back means to move back or away from something because you are frightened or shocked.

stare [stεər] v. 빤히 쳐다보다
If you stare at someone or something, you look at them for a long time.

lurch [lə:rtʃ] v. 갑자기 흔들리다
To lurch means to make a sudden movement, in an uncontrolled or unsteady way.

stumble [stʌmbl] v. 비틀거리다
If you stumble, you put your foot down awkwardly while you are walking or running and nearly fall over.

splash [splæʃ] v. 튀기다, 끼얹다
If you splash a liquid somewhere, it hits someone or something and scatters in small drops.

gasp [gæsp] v. 헉 하고 숨을 쉬다
When you gasp, you take a short quick breath through your mouth, especially when you are surprised or shocked.

damage [dǽmidʒ] v. 손상을 주다, 훼손하다
To damage an object means to break it, spoil it physically, or stop it from working properly.

glare [glεər] v. 노려보다
When you glare at someone, you look at them with an angry expression on your face.

shrug [ʃrʌg] n. 어깨를 으쓱하기
A shrug is an act of raising your shoulders and then dropping them to show that you do not know about something.

grumble [grʌmbl] v. 투덜거리다
If someone grumbles, they complain about something in a bad-tempered way.

neighborhood [néibərhùd] n. 지역, 장소
A neighborhood is a district or community within a town or city.

rent [rent] n. 임대, 임차
If something is for rent, it is available for you to use in exchange for a sum of money.

upscale [ʌ́pskèil] a. 고급의
An upscale place or product is one that is expensive and intended for people who are wealthy or belong to a high social class.

widen [waidn] v. (놀람 등으로) 둥그레지다
If your eyes widen, they open more.

hopeful [hóupfəl] a. 희망을 품은, 기대에 부푼
A hopeful action is one that you do in the hope that you will get what you want to get.

set on fire idiom ~에 불을 지르다
If you set something on fire, you make it start burning in order to damage or destroy it.

buzzer [bʌ́zər] n. 초인종
A buzzer is an electrical device that is used to make a long sound as a signal.

instantly [ínstəntli] ad. 즉시
If something happens instantly, it happens at once.

smolder [smóuldər] v. (서서히) 타다
If something smolders, it burns slowly, producing smoke but not flames.

slam [slæm] v. 쾅 닫다; n. 쾅 하는 소리
If you slam a door or window or if it slams, it shuts noisily and with great force.

discouraged [diskə́:ridʒd] a. 낙심한
If someone is discouraged, they are made to feel less confident, enthusiastic, and positive about something.

run-down [rʌn-dáun] a. 황폐한
A run-down building or area is in very poor condition.

dejected [didʒéktid] a. 낙담한
If you are dejected, you feel miserable or unhappy, especially because you have just been disappointed by something.

give up idiom 포기하다
If you give up, you decide that you cannot do something and stop trying to do it.

spot [spat] v. 발견하다
If you spot something or someone, you notice them.

shabby [ʃǽbi] a. 허름한
If you describe a person or thing as shabby, you mean that they look old and in bad condition.

flicker [flíkər] v. 스치다
If an emotion or expression flickers on someone's face or through their mind, it exists or is shown for only a short time.

chest [ʧest] n. 가슴
Your chest is the top part of the front of your body where your ribs, lungs, and heart are.

structure [strʌ́kʧər] n. 건축물
A structure is something that has been built or constructed, especially something big such as a building or bridge.

race [reis] v. (머리·심장 등이) 바쁘게 돌아가다
If your mind races, you think very fast about something because you are afraid or excited.

shrine [ʃrain] n. 제단, 사당
A shrine is a place where people come to worship because it is connected with a holy person or event.

snack [snæk] n. 간식
A snack is something such as a chocolate bar that you eat between meals.

souvenir [sùːvəníər] n. 기념품
A souvenir is an object that you buy or keep to remind you of a holiday, place, or event.

inspired [inspáiərd] a. 영감을 받은
If a book, work of art, or action is inspired by something, that thing is the source of the idea for it.

homeland [hóumlænd] n. 고향
Your homeland is your native country or region, especially the one in which you or your ancestors were born.

drip [drip] v. 떨어지다
When liquid drips somewhere, or you drip it somewhere, it falls in individual small drops.

barely [béərli] ad. 가까스로
You use barely to say that something is only just true or only just the case.

pace [peis] v. 왔다갔다하다
If you pace a small area, you keep walking up and down it, because you are anxious or impatient.

basement [béismənt] n. 지하실
A basement of a building is a room or floor that is built partly or entirely below ground level.

holler [hálər] v. 소리지르다, 고함치다
If you holler, you shout loudly.

splinter [splíntər] n. 조각, 파편
A splinter is a small thin sharp piece that has broken off a larger piece.

relief [rilí:f] n. 안도, 안심
Relief is the feeling of happiness that you have when something unpleasant stops or does not happen.

hearth [ha:rθ] n. 난로
The hearth is the floor of a fireplace, and the area in front of it.

cozy [kóuzi] a. 아늑한
If you say that a place is cozy, you mean it is nice, light, and comfortable.

give birth idiom 출산하다
When a woman or an animal gives birth, she produces a baby from her body.

light up idiom 환하게 만들다
If you light something up, it becomes bright, usually when you shine light on it.

murmur [mə́:rmə] v. 중얼거리다
If you murmur something, you say it very quietly so that not many people can hear what you are saying.

scoop [sku:p] v. 푸다, 뜨다
If you scoop something up, you put your hands or arms under it and lift it in a quick movement.

pour [pɔ:r] v. 붓다, 쏟다
If you pour a liquid or other substance, you make it flow steadily out of a container by holding the container at an angle.

coo [ku:] v. 옹알거리며 즐거워하다
When someone coos, they make a soft, pleasant sound, typically a sound of affection or happiness.

sneeze [sni:z] v. 재채기하다
When you sneeze, you suddenly blow air out through your nose and mouth without being able to stop it.

adjust [ədʒʌst] v. 적응하다
When you adjust to a new situation, you change your ideas or behavior in order to deal with it successfully.

custom [kʌ́stəm] n. 관습, 풍습
A custom is an activity, a way of behaving, or an event which is usual or traditional in a particular society or in particular circumstances.

cauldron [kɔ́:ldrən] n. 솥, 큰 냄비
A cauldron is a very large, round metal pot used for cooking over a fire.

blaze [bleiz] v. 이글거리다
If someone's eyes are blazing with an emotion, their eyes look very bright because they are feeling that emotion so strongly.

strength [streŋkθ] n. 힘
Your strength is the physical energy that you have, which gives you the ability to perform various actions, such as lifting or moving things.

flex one's muscle idiom 근육에 힘을 주다
If you flex your muscles, you pull your muscle tight to show someone how powerful you are, and show off your strength or power.

strike a pose idiom 포즈를 취하다
If you strike a pose, you hold your body in a particular way in order to attract attention.

silly [síli] a. 우스꽝스러운
If you say that someone or something is silly, you mean that they are foolish, childish, or ridiculous.

giggle [gigl] v. 피식 웃다, 킥킥거리다
If someone giggles, they laugh in a childlike way, because they are amused, nervous, or embarrassed.

cheer [ʧiər] v. 응원하다
When you cheer someone on, you shout loudly in order to encourage them, for example when they are taking part in a game.

take shape idiom 형태를 갖추다
When something takes shape, it develops or starts to appear in such a way that it becomes fairly clear what its final form will be.

shelving [ʃélviŋ] n. 선반, 책장
Shelving is a structure that can hold items on different levels.

repair [ripéər] v. 수리하다
If you repair something that has been damaged or is not working properly, you fix it.

eager [í:gər] a. 열망하는
If you are eager to do or have something, you want to do or have it very much.

ladder [lǽdər] n. 사다리
A ladder is a piece of equipment for reaching high places that consists of two bars and smaller pieces to be used as steps.

entrance [éntrəns] n. 입구
An entrance is a place where you can enter a building or a place.

strive [straiv] v. 노력하다, 애쓰다
If you strive to do something or strive for something, you make a great effort to do it or get it.

take over idiom ~을 이어받다
If you take over a company, you get control of it.

1 & 2

1. **When Ember was young, what did she do while her father rang up the order?**
   A. She stocked the shelves.
   B. She filled the lava java pot.
   C. She helped a customer looking for a product.
   D. She played with her toy cash register.

2. **How were kol nuts made?**
   A. The logs were cut with a knife.
   B. The logs were squeezed using palms.
   C. The logs were fried with oil.
   D. The logs were frozen and then cut.

3. How did Ember react when a customer insisted on getting a free sparkler?

A. She called her father for help.

B. She laughed and gave it to him.

C. She got angry and exploded.

D. She asked the customer to leave.

4. What did Ember recall when she had a difficult customer?

A. Her father's advice to stay calm

B. The time she exploded

C. The time she successfully handled a difficult customer

D. Her childhood days in the shop

5. What did Bernie do when Ember failed to handle the customer?

A. He made Ember to stay home for a week.

B. He made a new batch for the customer.

C. He yelled and exploded as well.

D. He took Ember to another room to scold her.

CHAPTER 1

Check Your Reading Speed

1분에 몇 단어를 읽는지 리딩 속도를 측정해 보세요.

$$\frac{1,086 \text{ words}}{\text{reading time ( ) sec}} \times 60 = (\quad) \text{ WPM}$$

Build Your Vocabulary

lava [láːvə] n. 용암
Lava is the very hot liquid rock that comes out of a volcano.

log [lɔːg] n. 통나무
A log is a piece of a thick branch or of the trunk of a tree that has been cut so that it can be used for fuel or for making things.

warmer [wɔ́ːrmər] n. 보온기
A warmer is something that keeps another thing warm.

counter [káuntər] n. 계산대
In a place such as a shop or café, a counter is a long narrow table or flat surface at which customers are served.

stock [stak] v. 채우다
To stock something such as a shelf or a shop means to fill it with goods or supplies.

shelf [ʃelf] n. (pl. shelves) 선반
A shelf is a flat piece of wood, plastic, or glass that is attached to the wall or is part of a piece of furniture, used for putting things on.

nearby [nìərbái] ad. 인근에, 가까운 곳에
If something is nearby, it is only a short distance away.

element [éləmənt] n. 원소
An element is one of the four substances (earth, air, fire, and water) from which people used to believe that everything was made.

greet [griːt] v. 인사하다, 맞이하다
To greet someone means to say hello to them or to welcome them.

authentic [ɔːθéntik] a. 진짜인, 진정한
If you describe something as authentic, it is made in the traditional or original way.

ring up idiom (상점에서 금전 등록기에 상품 가격을) 입력하다
If a shop assistant rings up a sale on a cash register, he or she presses the keys in order to record the amount that is being spent.

tap [tæp] v. 두드리다
When you tap something, you hit it with a quick, light blow or series of blows.

cash register [kǽʃ rèdʒistər] n. (금전) 등록기
A cash register is a machine in a shop, bar, or restaurant that is used for storing money and calculating the cost of what someone has bought.

squeeze [skwi:z] v. (꼭) 쥐다, 짜다
When you squeeze something, you press it firmly, usually with your hands.

palm [pa:m] n. 손바닥
The palm of your hand is the inside part of your hand, between your fingers and your wrist.

bite-sized [báit-sàizd] a. 한입 크기의
If you describe food as bite-sized, you mean it is small enough to be put whole into your mouth.

plate [pleit] n. 접시
A plate is a round or oval flat dish that is used to hold food.

announce [ənáuns] v. 큰 소리로 알리다
To announce means to say something in a loud and often serious way.

pride [praid] n. 자부심
Pride is a feeling of satisfaction which you have because you or people close to you have done something good or possess something good.

tousle [tauzl] v. 헝클어뜨리다
If you tousle something, you make it untidy.

flame [fleim] n. 불꽃
A flame is the hot, bright, and burning gas produced by something on fire.

emigrate [émigrèit] v. 이주하다
If you emigrate, you leave your own country to live in another country.

district [dístrikt] n. 구역
A district is a particular area of a town or country.

assist [əsíst] v. 돕다
To assist someone means to help them do a job or task by doing part of the work for them.

delivery [dilívəri] n. 배달
Delivery is the act of taking goods or letters to the person or the place they have been sent to.

ride on one's shoulders idiom ~의 어깨 위에 올라타다, 목마를 타다
If a small child rides on your shoulders, they sit there as you move along.

buzz around idiom 분주하게 돌아다니다
If you buzz around, you move around quickly, especially because you are very busy.

echo [ékou] v. 그대로 따라 하다
If you echo someone's words, you repeat them or express agreement with their attitude or opinion.

lollipop [lálipàp] n. 막대 사탕 (= pop)
A lollipop is a hard round or flat sweet made of boiled sugar on a small stick.

approach [əpróuʧ] v. 다가가다, 접근하다
To approach something means to get closer to it.

melt [melt] v. 녹이다
When a solid substance melts or when you melt it, it changes to a liquid, usually because it has been heated.

sculpt [skʌlpt] v. 형태를 만들다
When you sculpt something, you shape it in a skillful way.

inner [ínər] a. 내부의
Inner is used to describe something that is inside or contained within something else.

glow [glou] v. 빛나다
When something glows, it produces a steady light.

halo [héilou] n. 후광
A halo is a circle of light round a person or thing, or something that looks like a circle of light.

shimmer [ʃímər] v. 희미하게 빛나다
When light shimmers somewhere, it shines with a soft, changing light, but does not give a clear image.

tweak [twi:k] v. 잡아당기다
If you tweak something, especially part of someone's body, you hold it between your finger and thumb and twist it or pull it.

delight [diláit] n. 기쁨, 즐거움
A delight is a feeling of very great pleasure.

lean [li:n] v. (몸을) 숙이다
When you lean in a particular direction, you bend your body in that direction.

lick [lik] v. 핥다
When people or animals lick something, they move their tongue across its surface.

snap [snæp] v. 날카롭게 말하다
When you snap, you say something in a quick, angry way.

track [træk] v. 발자국을 남기다
When you track something such as mud or dirt, you leave dirty marks behind you as you walk.

carelessly [kéərlisli] ad. 부주의하게
If you do something carelessly, you do it without care or effort.

bump [bʌmp] v. 부딪치다
If you bump into something or someone, you accidentally hit them while you are moving.

nod [nad] v. (고개를) 끄덕이다
If you nod, you move your head up and down to show agreement, understanding, or approval.

mutter [mʌ́tər] v. 중얼거리다
If you mutter, you speak very quietly so that you cannot easily be heard, often because you are complaining about something.

keep an eye on idiom ~을 감시하다
To keep an eye on something means to watch it carefully so that it does not harm someone.

protective [prətéktiv] a. 보호용의
Something that is protective is designed to protect or shield from harm, damage, or injury.

armor [á:rmər] n. 갑옷
Armor is a special clothing that people wear to protect their bodies.

salute [səlúːt] v. 경례하다
When you salute someone, you greet or show respect to them, often by raising your hand to your forehead.

pour [pɔːr] v. 붓다, 쏟다
If you pour a liquid or other substance, you make it flow steadily out of a container by holding the container at an angle.

flaming [fléimiŋ] a. 불타는
Flaming describes something that is burning or on fire.

souvenir [sùːvəníər] n. 기념품
A souvenir is an object that you buy or keep to remind you of a holiday, place, or event.

giggle [gigl] v. 피식 웃다, 킥킥거리다
If someone giggles, they laugh in a childlike way, because they are amused, nervous, or embarrassed.

sputter [spʌ́tər] v. (불꽃 따위가) 탁탁 튀다; 식식거리며 말하다
If something such as a flame sputters, it makes a series of soft explosive sounds.

blaze [bleiz] v. 활활 타다
When a fire blazes, it burns strongly and brightly.

splash [splæʃ] v. 튀기다, 끼얹다
If you splash a liquid somewhere, it hits someone or something and scatters in small drops.

growl [graul] v. 으르렁거리듯 말하다
If someone growls something, they say something in a low, rough, and angry voice.

pop [pap] v. 갑자기 움직이다
If something pops, it moves quickly and suddenly, especially out of something.

in time idiom 시간 맞춰, 늦지 않게
If you are in time for a particular event, you are not too late for it.

slosh [slaʃ] v. 철벅거리다
If a liquid sloshes around, it moves in a noisy or messy way.

satisfied [sǽtisfàid] a. 만족스러운
If you are satisfied, it means you are pleased because you have what you want, or because something has happened in the way that you want.

holler [hálər] v. 소리지르다, 고함치다
If you holler, you shout loudly.

water down idiom ~을 약화시키다
If you water down something, you make it less effective or powerful.

restock [risták] v. 다시 채우다, 보충하다
If you restock something such as a shelf, fridge, or shop, you fill it with food or other goods to replace what you have used or sold.

dramatically [drəmǽtikəli] ad. 과장되게
You use dramatically to say that something is done in a very big way to get a lot of attention.

hang on one's every word idiom ~의 말을 귀 기울여 듣다
If you hang on someone's every word, you listen very carefully to what they are saying.

glance [glæns] v. 흘낏 보다
If you glance at something or someone, you look at them very quickly and then look away again immediately.

gasp [gæsp] v. 헉 하고 숨을 쉬다
When you gasp, you take a short quick breath through your mouth, especially when you are surprised or shocked.

boast [boust] v. 자랑하며 말하다
If you boast, you talk with excessive pride and self-satisfaction about your achievements, possessions, or abilities.

struggle [strʌgl] v. 노력하다, 애쓰다
If you struggle to do something, you try hard to do it, even though other people or things may be making it difficult for you to succeed.

compress [kəmprés] v. 압축하다
If you compress something, you press them and make them smaller.

effortlessly [éfərtlisli] ad. 수월하게
If something is done effortlessly, it is done easily.

stack [stæk] v. 쌓다
If you stack a number of things, you arrange them in neat piles.

pile [pail] n. 더미
A pile of things is a mass of them that is high in the middle and has sloping sides.

nudge [nʌdʒ] v. (팔꿈치로) 쿡 찌르다
If you nudge someone, you push them gently, usually with your elbow, in order to draw their attention to something.

hesitate [hézətèit] v. 망설이다, 주저하다
If you hesitate, you do not speak or act for a short time, usually because you are uncertain, embarrassed, or worried about what you are going to say or do.

beam [bi:m] v. 환하게 웃다
If you beam, you smile very happily.

wipe [waip] v. 닦다
If you wipe something, you rub its surface to remove dirt or liquid from it.

apron [éiprən] n. 앞치마
An apron is a piece of clothing that you put on over the front of your normal clothes and tie round your waist.

take a breath idiom 심호흡을 하다
If you say that you took a breath before doing something dangerous or frightening, you mean that you tried to make yourself feel strong and confident.

bucket [bʌ́kit] n. 양동이, 들통
A bucket is a round metal or plastic container with a handle attached to its sides.

sparkler [spáːrklər] n. (손에 들고 터뜨리는) 폭죽
A sparkler is a small firework that you can hold as it burns.

grab [græb] v. 움켜잡다
If you grab something, you take it or pick it up suddenly and roughly.

nervously [nə́ːrvəsli] ad. 초조하게
If you do something nervously, you do it while feeling worried or not relaxed.

gently [dʒéntli] ad. 부드럽게
Gently means in a kind, mild, or careful manner.

grip [grip] n. 움켜쥠
A grip is a firm, strong hold on something.

insist [insíst] v. 우기다, 고집하다
To insist means to demand that something must be done or that you must have a particular thing.

plaster on a smile idiom 억지 웃음을 짓다
If you plaster on a smile, you smile even though you are not happy.

bouquet [boukéi] n. 다발
A bouquet of things is a number of things, especially a large number.

burned-out [bə̀:rnd-áut] a. 타버린
If something is burned-out, it is badly damaged by fire that they can no longer be used.

demand [dimǽnd] v. 요구하다
If you demand something such as information or action, you ask for it in a very forceful way.

bellow [bélou] v. 고함치다
To bellow means to shout in a deep, loud voice.

flicker [flíkər] v. (불·빛 등이) 깜박거리다
If a light or flame flickers, it shines unsteadily.

explode [iksplóud] v. 폭발하다
If an object such as a bomb explodes or if someone or something explodes it, it bursts loudly and with great force, often causing damage or injury.

blast [blæst] n. 폭발
A blast is a big explosion, especially one caused by a bomb.

clear [kliər] v. (연기 등이) 걷히다
When fog or mist clears, it slowly disappears.

smoky [smóuki] a. 연기가 나는
Smoky describes something filled with or smelling of smoke.

blob [blab] n. 덩어리
A blob is a small amount of a thick liquid.

scorch mark [skɔ́:rʧ ma:rk] n. 검게 탄 자국
A scorch mark is a mark made on a surface by burning.

streak [stri:k] v. 기다란 자국을 내다, 줄무늬를 넣다
If something streaks a surface, it makes long stripes or marks on the surface.

stick [stik] v. (stuck-stuck) 꽂다, 찌르다
If you stick something long and thin into something else, you push them into it.

melty [mélti] a. 녹기 시작한
If something is melty, it is at a soft and partly liquid state due to heat.

lose one's temper idiom 화를 내다
If you lose your temper, you become so angry that you shout at someone or show in some other way that you are no longer in control of yourself.

tough [tʌf] a. 굽힐 줄 모르는, 다루기 힘든
Tough customer means someone who is difficult to deal with because they are very determined to do what they want.

connection [kənékʃən] n. 연결, 관계
A connection is a relationship between two things, people, or groups.

take over idiom ~을 이어받다
If you take over a company, you get control of it.

CHAPTER 2

Check Your Reading Speed
1분에 몇 단어를 읽는지 리딩 속도를 측정해 보세요.

$$\frac{587 \text{ words}}{\text{reading time ( ) sec}} \times 60 = (\quad) \text{ WPM}$$

Build Your Vocabulary

recall [rikɔ́ːl] v. 상기하다
If you recall something, you bring it back into your mind and remember it.

take a breath idiom 심호흡을 하다
If you say that you took a breath before doing something dangerous or frightening, you mean that you tried to make yourself feel strong and confident.

connection [kənékʃən] n. 연결, 관계
A connection is a relationship between two things, people, or groups.

lick [lik] n. 소량
A lick of something is a small amount of it.

explode [iksplóud] v. 폭발하다
If an object such as a bomb explodes or if someone or something explodes it, it bursts loudly and with great force, often causing damage or injury.

smash [smæʃ] v. 부수다
If you smash something, it breaks into many pieces, for example when it is hit or dropped.

countertop [káuntərtàp] n. 주방용 조리대
A countertop is a flat working surface, typically in a shop, used for various activities such as food preparation or serving customers.

cast [kæst] v. (cast-cast) (시선·미소 등을) 던지다
If you cast your eyes or cast a look in a particular direction, you look quickly in that direction.

apologetic [əpàlədʒétik] a. 미안해하는
If you are apologetic, you show or say that you are sorry for causing trouble for someone.

embarrassed [imbǽrəst] a. 당황스러운
A person who is embarrassed feels shy, ashamed, or guilty about something.

regular [régjulər] n. 단골손님
The regulars at a place or in a team are the people who often go to the place or are often in the team.

batch [bætʃ] n. 한 회분
A batch refers to a quantity or group of items or objects that are processed or produced together.

on the house idiom 무료로 제공되는
If something is on the house, you do not have to pay for it.

nod [nad] v. (고개를) 끄덕이다
If you nod, you move your head up and down to show agreement, understanding, or approval.

turn on one's heel idiom 휙 돌아서다
To turn on one's heel means to quickly turn around and walk away, typically due to a sudden change of mind or a negative reaction.

scoop [sku:p] v. 푸다, 뜨다
If you scoop something up, you put your hands or arms under it and lift it in a quick movement.

chew [tʃu:] v. 씹다
When you chew food, you use your teeth to break it up in your mouth so that it becomes easier to swallow.

tense [tens] a. 긴장한
If you are tense, you are anxious and nervous and cannot relax.

broil [brɔil] n. 흥분 상태
If someone is at a broil, they are very heated or angry.

admit [ædmít] v. 인정하다
If you admit something, you agree, often unwillingly, that it is true.

glow [glou] v. 빛나다
When something glows, it produces a steady light.

flatten [flætn] v. 납작하게 만들다
If you flatten something, you make something more even and smooth by getting rid of any bumps.

pane [pein] n. 판유리
A pane is a flat piece of glass or transparent material, often used in windows or doors.

inhale [inhéil] n. 들이마시기
An inhale is the act of breathing in or taking air into the lungs.

touch [tʌʧ] n. 마무리 작업, 손질
A touch is a small detail that is added to something in order to improve it or make it complete.

slide [slaid] v. (slid-slid) 슬며시 움직이다
When you slide something somewhere, it moves there smoothly over or against something.

satisfied [sǽtisfàid] a. 만족스러운
If you are satisfied, it means you are pleased because you have what you want, or because something has happened in the way that you want.

sigh [sai] n. 한숨
A sigh is a slow breath out that makes a long soft sound, especially because you are disappointed, tired, annoyed, or relaxed.

cough [kɔːf] v. 기침하다; n. 기침
When you cough, you force air out of your throat with a sudden, harsh noise.

sniff [snif] v. 코를 훌쩍이다
When you sniff, you draw air into your nose audibly and with force.

insist [insíst] v. 우기다, 고집하다
To insist means to demand that something must be done or that you must have a particular thing.

catch one's breath idiom 한숨 돌리다
When you catch your breath while you are doing something energetic, you stop for a short time so that you can start breathing normally again.

terrible [térəbl] a. 심한
If something is terrible, it is very bad or of very poor quality.

put someone out of one's misery idiom ~에게 속 편하게 말해 주다
If you put someone out of their misery, you tell them something that they are very anxious to know.

retire [ritáiər] v. 은퇴하다
When people retire, they leave their job and usually stop working completely.

crack a joke idiom 농담하다
If you crack a joke, you tell it.

disappointment [disəpɔ́intmənt] n. 실망
Disappointment the feeling of being sad because something has not happened or been as good or successful as you expected.

burst [bə:rst] v. (burst-burst) 갑자기 ~하다
If you burst into tears, laughter, or song, you suddenly begin to cry, laugh, or sing.

delivery [dilívəri] n. 배달
Delivery is the act of taking goods or letters to the person or the place they have been sent to.

echo [ékou] v. 그대로 따라 하다
If you echo someone's words, you repeat them or express agreement with their attitude or opinion.

beat [bi:t] v. (기록을) 깨뜨리다
If someone beats a record or achievement, they do better than it.

crank [kræŋk] v. [기계] 크랭크를 돌려 작동시키다
If you crank an engine or machine, you make it move or function, especially by turning a handle.

smokestack [smóukstæk] n. 굴뚝
A smokestack is a very tall chimney that carries smoke away from a factory.

tick [tik] v. 똑딱거리다
When a clock or watch ticks, it makes a regular series of short sounds as it works.

pack [pæk] v. (짐을) 싸다
If you pack up your things, you put your possessions or the things you have been using in a case or bag, because you are leaving.

3 & 4

1. **What happened when Ember took the flower from Clod?**

   A. She bloomed even more.

   B. She gave it back to Clod.

   C. It burned up in her hand.

   D. More flowers sprouted from Clod.

2. **Why didn't Ember want to leave her part of town?**

   A. She did not like the people from other parts of town.

   B. She had all she needed, and the city was not for Fire people.

   C. She was scared of Wetro train.

   D. The road outside town was not suitable for her scooter.

3. Why hadn't Bernie been able to retire?

A. Ember was not ready to take over.

B. He wanted to continue his job.

C. The family needed money.

D. He could still make kol nuts.

4. How did Ember react when the crowd of customers was waiting outside the shop?

A. She hid in the basement.

B. She made more kolnuts.

C. She stayed calm.

D. She called Bernie for help.

5. Why did Ember need to take a break from the shop?

A. Because she was too tired

B. Because she was angry

C. Because she needed to have lunch

D. Because she needed to fix a pipe

CHAPTER 3

Check Your Reading Speed

1분에 몇 단어를 읽는지 리딩 속도를 측정해 보세요.

$$\frac{1{,}299 \text{ words}}{\text{reading time ( ) sec}} \times 60 = (\quad) \text{ WPM}$$

Build Your Vocabulary

cozy [kóuzi] a. 아늑한
If you say that a place is cozy, you mean it is nice, light, and comfortable.

self-appointed [sèlf-əpɔ́intid] a. 자기가 정한, 자칭의
If someone is self-appointed, he or she has taken a position without anyone else asking them or choosing them to have it.

matchmaker [mǽʧmèikər] n. 중매인
A matchmaker is person who helps other people find someone they might be romantically interested in.

natural [nǽʧərəl] a. 타고난
Someone with a natural ability or skill was born with that ability and did not have to learn it.

gift [gift] n. 재능, 재주
If someone has a gift for doing something, they have a natural ability for doing it.

without a doubt idiom 의심할 바 없이
If you do something without a doubt, you emphasize that it is definitely true.

match [mæʧ] n. 어울리는 사람; v. 어울리다
If a combination of things or people is a good match, they have a pleasing effect when placed or used together.

gaze [geiz] v. 응시하다, 바라보다
To gaze at something or someone means to look steadily and intently, especially in admiration, surprise, or thought.

surface [sə́:rfis] n. 표면
When you refer to the surface of a situation, you are talking about what can be seen easily rather than what is hidden or not immediately obvious.

stir [stə:r] v. 휘젓다
If you stir a liquid or other substance, you move it around or mix it in a container using something such as a spoon.

sniff [snif] v. 냄새를 맡다
If you sniff something, you breathe air in through the nose in order to discover or enjoy the smell of it.

wisp [wisp] n. (연기·구름의) 줄기
A wisp of something such as smoke or cloud is an amount of it in a long thin shape.

dissipate [dísəpèit] v. 소멸되다
When something dissipates, it becomes less or becomes less strong until it goes away completely.

scold [skould] v. 야단치다
If you scold someone, you speak angrily to them because they have done something wrong.

grab [græb] v. 움켜잡다
If you grab something, you take it or pick it up suddenly and roughly.

go for idiom ~을 얻으려고 애쓰다
To go for something means to put a lot of effort into something, so that you get or achieve something.

race [reis] v. 급히 가다
If you race somewhere, you go there as quickly as possible.

announce [ənáuns] v. 큰 소리로 알리다
To announce means to say something in a loud and often serious way.

shoot [ʃu:t] v. (shot-shot) (눈길 등을) 휙 던지다
If you shoot a look at someone, you look at them quickly and briefly, often in a way that expresses your feelings.

confirm [kənfə́:rm] v. 확인해 주다
If you confirm something that has been stated or suggested, you say that it is true because you know about it.

sigh [sai] v. 한숨을 쉬다
When you sigh, you let out a deep breath, as a way of expressing feelings such as disappointment, tiredness, or pleasure.

dying wish idiom 죽기 전 소원
A dying wish refers to the final desire or request of a person before they die.

crackle [krǽkl] v. 탁탁 소리를 내다
If something crackles, it makes a rapid series of short, harsh noises.

remind [rimáind] v. 상기시키다
If someone reminds you of a fact or event that you already know about, they say something which makes you think about it.

embrace [imbréis] v. 포옹하다
If you embrace someone, you put your arms around them and hold them tightly, usually in order to show your love or affection for them.

squirt [skwəːrt] v. 찍 뿌리다
If you squirt a liquid somewhere, the liquid comes out of a narrow opening in a thin fast stream.

spray [sprei] n. 분무기
A spray is a piece of equipment for spraying water or another liquid, especially over growing plants.

spit [spit] v. (spat/spit-spat/spit) 내뱉듯이 말하다
If someone spits an insult or comment, they say it in an angry or hostile way.

sputter [spʌ́tər] v. 식식거리며 말하다
If you sputter, you speak with difficulty and make short sounds, especially because you are angry, shocked, or excited.

earth [əːrθ] n. 흙
Earth is the substance in which plants grow that covers most of the land.

pop [pap] v. 불쑥 나타나다
If someone or something pops, it appears suddenly or unexpectedly.

planter [plǽntər] n. 화분
A planter is a container, typically made of plastic or ceramic, used for growing plants.

sprout [spraut] v. 돋아나다, 자라다
When leaves, shoots, or plants sprout somewhere, they grow there.

comb [koum] n. 빗질
If you give your hair a comb, you make it tidy using a comb.

groan [groun] v. (고통·짜증으로) 신음 소리를 내다
If you groan something, you say it in a low, unhappy voice.

strap [stræp] v. 끈으로 묶다
If you strap something somewhere, you fasten it there with a strap.

bloom [blu:m] n. 개화(기), 활짝 필 때
Bloom is a period of flowering.

date [deit] n. 데이트 상대
A date is someone who you are having a romantic meeting with.

grown up idiom 다 큰, 어른이 된
Someone who is grown up is physically and mentally mature and no longer depends on their parents or another adult.

reveal [riví:l] v. 드러내 보이다
To reveal something means to make people aware of it.

armpit [á:rmpit] n. 겨드랑이
Your armpits are the areas of your body under your arms where your arms join your shoulders.

pluck [plʌk] v. (잡아 당겨) 빼내다
If you pluck something from somewhere, you take it between your fingers and pull it sharply from where it is.

let out idiom (소리를) 내다
If you let out a particular sound, you make that sound.

kneel [ni:l] v. (knelt-knelt) 무릎을 꿇다
When you kneel, you bend your legs so that your knees are touching the ground.

sidewalk [sáidwɔ:k] n. 보도
A sidewalk is a paved path for pedestrians beside a road.

grand [grænd] a. 당당한
If an action is described as grand, it is done in a really special and exciting way.

gesture [dʒésʧər] n. 몸짓
A gesture is a movement that you make with a part of your body.

burn to a crisp idiom 새까맣게 타다
If something burns to a crisp, it becomes completely burnt.

buddy [bʌ́di] n. 친구
Buddy is an informal term used to refer to a close friend or companion.

tick [tik] v. 똑딱거리다
When a clock or watch ticks, it makes a regular series of short sounds as it works.

beg [beg] v. 애원하다, 간청하다
If you beg someone to do something, you ask them very anxiously or eagerly to do it.

glance [glæns] v. 흘낏 보다
If you glance at something or someone, you look at them very quickly and then look away again immediately.

annoyed [ənɔ́id] a. 짜증난
If you are annoyed, you are fairly angry about something.

waggle [wǽgl] v. 흔들다, 움직거리다
If you waggle something, it moves up and down or from side to side with short quick movements.

eyebrow [áibràu] n. 눈썹
Your eyebrows are the lines of hair which grow above your eyes.

bother [báðər] v. 일부러 ~하다
If you do not bother to do something or if you do not bother with it, you do not do it, consider it, or use it because you think it is unnecessary.

grocery store [gróusəri stɔːr] n. 식료품 잡화점
A grocery store is a shop that sells food and other things used in the home.

delivery [dilívəri] n. 배달물
A delivery is the goods that are delivered.

rush [rʌʃ] v. 급히 움직이다
If you rush somewhere, you go there quickly.

deliver [dilívər] v. 배달하다
If you deliver something somewhere, you take it there.

package [pǽkidʒ] n. 소포
A package is an object or group of objects wrapped in paper or packed in a box.

stall [stɔːl] n. 가판대
A stall is a large table on which you put goods that you want to sell, or information that you want to give people.

charcoal [tʃáːrkòul] n. 숯
Charcoal is a black substance obtained by burning wood without much air.

lighter fluid [láitər flúːid] n. 라이터 연료
Lighter fluid is the liquid in a lighter that is its fuel.

lid [lid] n. 뚜껑
A lid is a cover for a container, such as a pot or box.

tiny [táini] a. 아주 작은
Tiny describes something that is very small in size or extent.

coal [koul] n. 석탄
Coal is a hard black substance that is extracted from the ground and burned as fuel.

suck [sʌk] v. 빨아 먹다
If you suck something, you hold it in your mouth and pull at it with the muscles in your cheeks and tongue.

burp [bəːrp] v. 트림하다
When someone burps, they make a noise because air from their stomach has been forced up through their throat.

tension [ténʃən] n. 긴장감
Tension is a feeling of nervousness that makes you unable to relax or emotional strain or suspense.

melt [melt] v. (감정 등이) 누그러지다
If something such as your feelings melt, they suddenly disappear and you no longer feel them.

traffic [trǽfik] n. 차량들, 교통(량)
Traffic refers to all the vehicles that are moving along the roads in a particular area.

patience [péiʃəns] n. 인내심
Patience is the ability to accept trouble and other people's annoying behavior without complaining or becoming angry.

rev [rev] v. (엔진의) 회전 속도를 올리다
When you rev a vehicle, the engine speed is increased.

maneuver [mənúːvər] v. 조종하다
To maneuver means to skillfully move or guide something.

fist [fist] n. 주먹
Your hand is referred to as your fist when you have bent your fingers in toward the palm in order to hit someone, to make an angry gesture, or to hold something.

parcel [páːrsəl] n. 소포
A parcel is package wrapped in paper or packed in a box.

firework [fáiərwəːrk] n. 폭죽
Fireworks are small objects that are lit to entertain people on special occasions.

swarm [swɔːrm] v. 몰려들다
When people swarm somewhere, they move there quickly in a large group.

delight [diláit] n. 기쁨, 즐거움
A delight is a feeling of very great pleasure.

light up idiom 환하게 만들다
If you light something up, it becomes bright, usually when you shine light on it.

go off idiom (경보기 등이) 울리다
If an alarm bell goes off, it makes a sudden loud noise.

asleep [əslíːp] a. 잠든
Someone who is asleep is sleeping.

counter [káuntər] n. 계산대
In a place such as a shop or café, a counter is a long narrow table or flat surface at which customers are served.

surround [səráund] v. 둘러싸다
If a person or thing is surrounded by something, that thing is located all around them.

paperwork [péipərwəːrk] n. 서류
Paperwork refers to all the documents that you need for a particular activity or occasion.

tone down idiom (어조 등을) 좀 더 누그러뜨리다
If you tone down something that you have written or said, you make it less forceful, severe, or offensive.

celebration [sèləbréiʃən] n. 축하
Celebration is the act of expressing joy and excitement about something.

tiptoe [típtòu] v. 발끝으로 걷다
If you tiptoe somewhere, you walk there very quietly without putting your heels on the floor when you walk.

fade [feid] v. 서서히 사라지다
If someone's smile fades, they slowly stop smiling.

retire [ritáiər] v. 은퇴하다
When people retire, they leave their job and usually stop working completely.

lose one's temper idiom 화를 내다
If you lose your temper, you become so angry that you shout at someone or show in some other way that you are no longer in control of yourself.

drape [dreip] v. 걸치다
If you drape a piece of cloth somewhere, you place it there so that it hangs down in a casual and graceful way.

chain mail [ʧéin meil] n. 쇠사슬 갑옷
Chain mail is a kind of armor made from small metal rings joined together so that they look like cloth.

smoky [smóuki] a. 연기가 나는
Smoky describes something filled with or smelling of smoke.

cough [kɔːf] n. 기침; v. 기침하다
A cough is an illness in which you cough often and your chest or throat hurts.

cheek [ʧiːk] n. 뺨, 볼
Your cheeks are the sides of your face below your eyes.

head [hed] v. (특정 방향으로) 가다
If you are heading for a particular place, you are going toward that place.

ring out idiom 크게 울리다
If a sound rings out, it can be heard loudly and clearly.

beat [biːt] v. (beat-beaten) (기록을) 깨뜨리다
If someone beats a record or achievement, they do better than it.

shrug [ʃrʌg] v. (어깨를) 으쓱하다
If you shrug, you raise your shoulders and then drop them to show that you do not know or care about something.

twig [twig] n. (나무의) 잔가지
A twig is a very small thin branch that grows out from a main branch of a tree or bush.

stack [stæk] n. 더미
A stack of things is a pile of them.

cauldron [kɔ́ːldrən] n. 솥, 큰 냄비
A cauldron is a very large, round metal pot used for cooking over a fire.

sleep in idiom 늦잠을 자다
If you sleep in, it means to stay in bed longer than usual, especially in the morning.

by oneself idiom 도움을 받지 않고
If you do something by yourselves, you succeed in doing it without anyone helping you.

challenge [ʧǽlindʒ] v. (시합 등을) 제의하다
To challenge someone means to strongly suggest that they do something.

toss [tɔːs] v. 던지다
If you toss something, you throw it into the air with a quick, forceful motion.

let down idiom ~을 실망시키다
If you let someone down, you disappoint them, by not doing something that you have said you will do or that they expected you to do.

swear [swɛər] v. 맹세하다
If you swear to do something, you promise in a serious way that you will do it.

pat [pæt] v. 쓰다듬다, 토닥거리다
If you pat something or someone, you tap them lightly, usually with your hand held flat.

trudge [trʌdʒ] v. 터덜터덜 걷다
If you trudge somewhere, you walk there slowly and with heavy steps, especially because you are tired or unhappy.

whisper [hwíspər] v. 속삭이다
When you whisper, you say something very quietly, using your breath rather than your throat, so that only one person can hear you.

go one's way idiom 자기 생각대로 하다
If an event goes your way, it happens in the way you want.

Check Your Reading Speed

1분에 몇 단어를 읽는지 리딩 속도를 측정해 보세요.

$$\frac{1{,}232 \text{ words}}{\text{reading time ( ) sec}} \times 60 = (\ ) \text{ WPM}$$

Build Your Vocabulary

slap [slæp] v. 재빨리 붙이다
If you slap something onto a surface, you put it there quickly, roughly, or carelessly.

adjust [ədʒʌ́st] v. (매무새 등을) 바로잡다
If you adjust something such as your clothing or a machine, you correct or alter its position or setting.

apron [éiprən] n. 앞치마
An apron is a piece of clothing that you put on over the front of your normal clothes and tie round your waist.

remind [rimáind] v. 상기시키다
If someone reminds you of a fact or event that you already know about, they say something which makes you think about it.

candle [kǽndl] n. 촛불
A candle is a stick of wax with string going through it that you burn to produce light.

keep one's cool idiom 침착함을 유지하다
If you keep your cool, you try to stay calm and not get upset or angry.

rush [rʌʃ] v. 급히 움직이다
If you rush somewhere, you go there quickly.

practically [prǽktikəli] ad. 사실상
You use practically to say that something that is almost or nearly the case.

trample [trǽmpl] v. 짓밟다
If someone tramples something, they step heavily and carelessly on it and damage it.

flame [fleim] n. 불꽃
A flame is the hot, bright, and burning gas produced by something on fire.

arrange [əréindʒ] v. 배열하다
When you arrange items, you place them in a specific order or pattern.

yank [jæŋk] v. 홱 잡아당기다
If you yank someone or something somewhere, you pull them there suddenly and with a lot of force.

wobble [wabl] v. 흔들리다
If something or someone wobbles, they make small movements from side to side, for example because they are unsteady.

heave [hiːv] v. 들어서 던지다
If you heave something heavy or difficult to move somewhere, you push, pull, or lift it using a lot of effort.

armload [áːrmlòud] n. 한 아름(의 양)
An armload of something is the amount of it that you can carry fairly easily.

grunt [grʌnt] v. 툴툴거리다, 불평하다
If you grunt, you make a low sound, especially because you are annoyed or not interested in something.

fragile [frǽdʒəl] a. 깨지기 쉬운
If something is fragile, it is easily damaged or broken.

sweep [swiːp] v. (swept-swept) 쓸어 모으다
If you sweep things off something, you push them off with a quick smooth movement of your arm.

shelf [ʃelf] n. 선반 위의 물건
A shelf of things is the contents of a shelf.

delicate [délikət] a. 부서지기 쉬운
If something is delicate, it is easy to harm, damage, or break.

shatter [ʃǽtər] v. 산산조각 나다
If something shatters or is shattered, it breaks into a lot of small pieces.

stifle [staifl] v. 억누르다, 꾹 참다
If you stifle a yawn or laugh, you prevent yourself from yawning or laughing.

yell [jel] n. 고함
A yell is a loud shout given by someone who is afraid or in pain.

log [lɔːg] n. 통나무
A log is a piece of a thick branch or of the trunk of a tree that has been cut so that it can be used for fuel or for making things.

blur [bləːr] n. (기억이) 흐릿한 것
A blur is something that you cannot remember clearly.

endless [éndlis] a. 끝없는
If you say that something is endless, you mean that it is very large or lasts for a very long time, and it seems as if it will never stop.

stream [striːm] n. (계속 이어진) 줄; v. 줄줄 흐르다
A stream of vehicles or people is a long moving line of them.

constant [kánstənt] a. 끊임없는
You use constant to describe something that happens all the time or is always there.

cash register [kǽʃ rèdʒistər] n. (금전) 등록기
A cash register is a machine in a shop, bar, or restaurant that is used for storing money and calculating the cost of what someone has bought.

count on idiom ~을 믿다, 의지하다
If you count on someone or count upon them, you rely on them to support you or help you.

policy [páləsi] n. 정책, 방침
A policy is a set of ideas or plans that is used as a basis for making decisions, especially in politics, economics, or business.

damage [dǽmidʒ] v. 손상을 주다, 훼손하다
To damage an object means to break it, spoil it physically, or stop it from working properly.

connection [kənékʃən] n. 연결, 관계
A connection is a relationship between two things, people, or groups.

grit [grit] v. 이를 악물다
If you grit your teeth, you press your upper and lower teeth tightly together, usually because you are angry about something.

kettle [ketl] n. 주전자
A kettle is a covered container that you use for boiling water.

release [rilíːs] v. 내뿜다; 놓아 주다
If something releases gas, heat, or a substance, it causes it to leave its container or the substance that it was part of and enter the surrounding atmosphere or area.

high-pitched [hài-pítʃt] a. (음이) 아주 높은
A high-pitched sound is high and sometimes also loud or unpleasant.

whistle [hwisl] n. 삑삑 하는 소리
A whistle is a loud sound produced by air or steam being forced through a small opening, or by something moving quickly through the air.

blow one's top idiom 머리끝까지 화가 나다
When someone blows their top, they become extremely angry.

strain [strein] v. 안간힘을 쓰다
If you strain to do something, you make a great effort to do it when it is difficult to do.

choke out idiom (목이 메어) 간신히 ~라고 말하다
To choke out means to say something great difficulty because you feel a strong emotion.

clamp [klæmp] v. 꽉 잡다
To clamp something in a particular place means to put it or hold it there firmly and tightly.

spark [spaːrk] n. 불꽃
A spark is a tiny bright piece of burning material that flies up from something that is burning.

make it idiom 가다
If you make it to somewhere, you succeed in reaching there.

basement [béismənt] n. 지하실
A basement of a building is a room or floor that is built partly or entirely below ground level.

let out idiom (소리를) 내다
If something or someone lets water, air, or breath out, they allow it to flow out or escape.

fiery [fáiəri] a. 불의, 화염의
If you describe something as fiery, you mean that it is burning strongly or contains fire.

blast [blæst] n. 폭발
A blast is a big explosion, especially one caused by a bomb.

clear [kliər] v. (연기 등이) 걷히다
When fog or mist clears, it slowly disappears.

pant [pænt] v. (숨을) 헐떡이다
If you pant, you breathe quickly and loudly with your mouth open, usually because you have been doing something energetic.

recover [rikʌ́vər] v. 회복하다
To recover is to return to a normal state of health, mind, or strength after a physical or mental illness, injury, or shock.

vibrate [váibreit] v. 흔들리다
When something vibrates, it shakes repeatedly and quickly, often felt as rhythmic movement.

groan [groun] v. 삐걱거리다
If something groans, it makes a loud sound when it moves.

squeal [skwi:l] v. 끼익 하는 소리를 내다
If someone or something squeals, they make a long, high-pitched sound.

crack [kræk] v. 갈라지다, 금이 가다
If something hard cracks, it becomes slightly damaged, with lines appearing on its surface.

duck [dʌk] v. 휙 수그리다
If you duck, you move your head or the top half of your body quickly downward to avoid something that might hit you, or to avoid being seen.

douse [daus] v. (불을) 끄다
If you douse a fire, you stop it burning by pouring a lot of water over it.

gush [gʌʃ] v. 솟구치다
When liquid gushes out of something, or when something gushes a liquid, the liquid flows out very quickly and in large quantities.

flood [flʌd] v. 물에 잠기게 하다
If something such as a river or a burst pipe floods an area that is usually dry or if the area floods, it becomes covered with water.

gasp [gæsp] v. 헉 하고 숨을 쉬다
When you gasp, you take a short quick breath through your mouth, especially when you are surprised or shocked.

brick [brik] n. 벽돌
Bricks are rectangular blocks of baked clay used for building walls, which are usually red or brown.

column [káləm] n. 기둥 (모양의 것)
A column is something that has a tall narrow shape.

shudder [ʃʌ́dər] v. 마구 흔들리다
If something shudders, it shakes suddenly and violently.

dodge [dadʒ] v. (몸을) 피하다, 비키다
If you dodge something, you avoid it by quickly moving aside or out of reach so that it cannot hit or reach you.

spray [sprei] n. 물보라
Spray is a lot of small drops of water which are being thrown into the air.

lid [lid] n. 뚜껑
A lid is a cover for a container, such as a pot or box.

float [flout] v. (물 위나 공중에서) 떠다니다, 흘러가다
If something or someone is floating in a liquid, they are in the liquid, on or just below the surface, and are being supported by it.

debris [dəbríː] n. 파편
Debris is pieces from something that has been destroyed or pieces of rubbish or unwanted material that are spread around.

sting [stiŋ] v. (stung-stung) 쏘다
If something stings you, you feel a sharp pain.

weld [weld] v. 용접하다
If you weld something, you join together pieces of metal by heating their edges and pressing them together.

edge [edʒ] n. 가장자리
The edge of something is the place or line where it stops, or the part of it that is furthest from the middle.

hold one's breath idiom 숨을 죽이다
If you say that someone is holding their breath, you mean that they are waiting anxiously or excitedly for something to happen.

grip [grip] n. 움켜쥠
A grip is a firm, strong hold on something.

stay put idiom 그대로 있다
If you stay put, you remain somewhere.

water-logged [wɔ́:tər-lɔ́:gd] a. 물에 잠긴, 흠뻑 젖은
If an object or a place is water-logged, it is really soaked and full of water.

panic [pǽnik] v. 어쩔 줄 모르다
If you panic or if someone panics you, you suddenly feel anxious or afraid, and act quickly and without thinking carefully.

replenish [ripléniʃ] v. 다시 채우다
If you replenish something, you make it full or complete again.

suck [sʌk] v. (공기 등을) 들이마시다; 빨아들이다
When you suck in air, you draw it into your mouth by contracting your muscles, typically in surprise or preparation for action.

fountain [fáuntən] v. 솟아오르다
If something fountains up, it bursts out and goes up into the air in a flowing manner.

bawl [bɔ́:l] v. (시끄럽게) 울어대다
If you say that a child is bawling, you are annoyed because it is crying loudly.

sniffle [snifl] v. 훌쩍거리다
When someone sniffles, they make soft, quiet sounds, usually because they are crying.

lap [læp] n. 무릎
Lap is the top part of your legs that forms a flat surface when you are sitting down.

splash [splæʃ] v. 튀기다, 끼얹다
If you splash a liquid somewhere, it hits someone or something and scatters in small drops.

wince [wins] v. 움찔하고 놀라다
When you wince, the muscles of your face tighten suddenly because you have felt a pain or have seen something unpleasant.

shield [ʃiːld] v. 보호하다, 가리다
When you shield something, you protect it from harm or danger.

demand [dimǽnd] v. 강력히 묻다
If you demand something such as information or action, you ask for it in a very forceful way.

sob [sab] v. 흐느끼며 말하다
If you sob something, you say it while you are crying.

leak [liːk] n. (액체·기체가) 새는 곳; v. 새다
A leak is a crack, hole, or other gap that a substance such as a liquid or gas can pass through.

muscular [mʌ́skjulur] a. 근육질의
A person who is muscular is very fit and strong, with firm muscles.

whisper [hwíspər] v. 속삭이다
When you whisper, you say something very quietly, using your breath rather than your throat, so that only one person can hear you.

squish [skwiʃ] v. 으깨다
To squish means to press hard on a person or a soft object or substance.

out of shape idiom 몸매가 엉망인
If something is out of shape, it is no longer in its proper or original shape, for example because it has been damaged or wrongly handled.

disappear [dìsəpíər] v. 사라지다
When someone or something disappears, you can no longer see them.

belly [béli] n. 배, 복부
The belly is the front part of a person's or animal's body, between the chest and legs.

plop [plap] v. 풍덩 소리를 내다
If something plops somewhere, it drops there with a soft, gentle sound.

plead [pliːd] v. 애원하다
To plead means to ask someone for something in a very strong and serious way.

impatient [impéiʃənt] a. 짜증난
If you are impatient, you are annoyed because you have to wait too long for something.

mess [mes] n. 엉망인 상태
If you say that something is a mess or in a mess, you think that it is in an untidy state.

straighten [streitn] v. (자세를) 바로 하다
When you straighten up, you make your body upright from a relaxed or bent position.

slosh [slaʃ] v. 철벅거리다
If a liquid sloshes around, it moves in a noisy or messy way.

ticket [tíkit] n. (벌금을 부과하는) 딱지
A ticket is an official piece of paper which orders you to pay a fine or to appear in court because you have committed a driving or parking offence.

inspector [inspéktər] n. 조사관
An inspector is a person, usually employed by a government agency, whose job is to find out whether people are obeying official regulations.

definitely [défənitli] ad. 분명히
You use definitely to emphasize that something is the case, or to emphasize the strength of your intention or opinion.

up to code idiom 기준에 맞는
Up to code means everything is in working order and meets a checklist that someone must do to complete the job.

ironic [airánik] a. 모순적인
If you say that it is ironic that something should happen, you mean that it is odd or amusing because it involves a contrast.

poke [pouk] v. 쿡 찌르다
If you poke at something, you make lots of little pushing movements at it with a sharp object.

rumble [rʌmbl] v. 우르릉거리는 소리를 내다
If someone or something rumbles, it makes a low, continuous noise.

solid [sálid] a. 단단한
Solid means firm, strong, or not easily broken.

confirm [kənfə́:rm] v. 확인해 주다
If you confirm something that has been stated or suggested, you say that it is true because you know about it.

with one's bare hands idiom (도구 없이) 맨손으로
If someone does something with their bare hands, they do it without using any weapons or tools.

pride [praid] n. 자부심
Pride is a feeling of satisfaction which you have because you or people close to you have done something good or possess something good.

ruin [ruːin] n. 폐허
The ruins of a building are the parts of it that remain after the rest has fallen down or been destroyed.

permit [pərmít] n. 허가증
A permit is an official document which says that you may do something.

weep [wiːp] v. 울다
If someone weeps, they cry.

gulp [gʌlp] v. 침을 꿀꺽 삼키다
If you gulp, you swallow air, often making a noise in your throat as you do so, because you are nervous or excited.

citation [saitéiʃən] n. 위반 딱지
A citation is an official order for someone to appear in court or pay a fine for doing something illegal.

shut down idiom (공장·가게의) 문을 닫다
If a factory or business shuts down or if someone shuts it down, work there stops or it no longer trades as a business.

flare [flɛər] v. 확 타오르다
When a fire flares up, it suddenly burns more intensely.

wail [weil] v. 울부짖다, 통곡하다
If someone wails, they make a long, loud, high-pitched sound because they are sad or in pain.

awful [ɔ́ːfəl] a. 끔찍한
If you say that something is awful, you think that they are not very good.

beg [beg] v. 애원하다, 간청하다
If you beg someone to do something, you ask them very anxiously or eagerly to do it.

lunge [lʌndʒ] v. 달려들다
If you lunge in a particular direction, you move in that direction suddenly and clumsily.

take it easy idiom 진정해라
If someone tells you to take it easy or take things easy, they mean that you should relax and not do very much at all.

scribble [skribl] v. 갈겨쓰다
If you scribble something, you write it quickly and roughly.

furiously [fjúəriəsli] ad. 격렬하게
When someone does something furiously, they do it with a lot of energy or effort.

city hall [siti hɔ́ːl] n. 시청
A city hall refers to the building that houses the administrative offices of a city.

shift [ʃift] n. 교대 근무 시간
If a group of factory workers, nurses, or other people work shifts, they work for a set period before being replaced by another group, so that there is always a group working. Each of these set periods is called a shift.

pour [pɔːr] v. 붓다, 쏟다
If you pour a liquid or other substance, you make it flow steadily out of a container by holding the container at an angle.

rip [rip] v. 떼어 내다
If you rip something away, you remove it quickly and forcefully.

blaze [bleiz] v. 활활 타다
When a fire blazes, it burns strongly and brightly.

chase [ʧeis] v. 뒤쫓다
If you chase after someone, you run or move quickly to catch up to them.

joint [dʒɔint] n. 연결 부위
A joint is the place where two things are fastened or fixed together.

5 & 6

1. What did Ember see when the train burst out of the tunnel?

A. Another tunnel

B. A reflection of herself

C. A giant waterfall

D. A Wetro staff

2. What did Wade do with his tickets at City Hall?

A. He gave them to Ember.

B. He loaded them into a vacuum tube.

C. He let it flow onto a river.

D. He lost them on the way to city hall.

3. What did Ember do when kids blocked her path?

A. She used a ladder to climb a wall.

B. She used chili oil from a cart.

C. She floated over them.

D. She jumped really high.

4. What did Ember find when she returned to the shop?

A. The shop was closed, and there was a mess in the basement.

B. She saw customers crowding around the shop.

C. Bernie was preparing for the Red Dot Sale.

D. Everything was clean and organized.

5. Why did Ember's parents leave Fire Land?

A. They wanted to go on an adventure.

B. A great storm destroyed their restaurant.

C. They did not like the neighbors.

D. They were kicked out by Bernie's father.

Check Your Reading Speed

1분에 몇 단어를 읽는지 리딩 속도를 측정해 보세요.

$$\frac{994 \text{ words}}{\text{reading time ( ) sec}} \times 60 = (\quad) \text{ WPM}$$

Build Your Vocabulary

chase [ʧeis] v. 뒤쫓다
If you chase after someone, you run or move quickly to catch up to them.

aloud [əláud] ad. 큰 소리로
When you say something, read, or laugh aloud, you speak or laugh so that other people can hear you.

board [bɔːrd] v. 탑승하다
When you board a train, ship, or aircraft, you get on it in order to travel somewhere.

element [éləmənt] n. 원소
An element is one of the four substances (earth, air, fire, and water) from which people used to believe that everything was made.

announcer [ənáunsər] n. (역·공항 등에서) 안내 방송을 하는 사람
An announcer is a person who gives information about something in a station, an airport.

ring out idiom 크게 울리다
If a sound rings out, it is loud and clear enough to be heard by everyone around.

scan [skæn] v. (유심히) 살피다
When you scan a place or a group of people, you look at it carefully, usually because you are looking for something or someone.

squeeze [skwiːz] v. 비집고 들어가다
If you squeeze a person or thing somewhere or if they squeeze there, they manage to get through or into a small space.

grassy [grǽsi] a. 풀이 무성한
If something is grassy, it means it is covered with a lot of soft green plants.

lurch [ləːrʧ] v. 갑자기 흔들리다
To lurch means to make a sudden movement in an uncontrolled or unsteady way.

accidentally [æksədéntəli] ad. 우연히, 뜻하지 않게
If something occurs accidentally, it happens in an accidental or unintended manner.

slam [slæm] v. 부딪치다
If one thing slams into or against another, it crashes into it with great force.

skinny [skíni] a. 비쩍 마른
If you are skinny, you are very thin.

spot [spat] v. 발견하다
If you spot something or someone, you notice them.

crowded [kráudid] a. 붐비는
If a place is crowded, it is full of people.

inch [inʧ] v. 조금씩 움직이다
To inch somewhere means to move there very slowly and carefully.

whip [hwip] v. 갑자기 움직이게 하다
If something, for example the wind, whips something, it strikes it sharply.

splash [splæʃ] v. 철벅 떨어지다
If a liquid splashes, it hits someone or something and scatters in a lot of small drops.

aqueduct [ǽkwədʌkt] n. 수로교
An aqueduct is a long bridge with many arches, which carries a water supply or a canal over a valley.

waterfall [wɔ́ːtərfɔːl] n. 폭포
A waterfall is a place where water flows over the edge of a steep, high cliff in hills or mountains, and falls into a pool below.

in time idiom 시간 맞춰, 늦지 않게
If you are in time for a particular event, you are not too late for it.

catch one's breath idiom 한숨 돌리다
When you catch your breath while you are doing something energetic, you stop for a short time so that you can start breathing normally again.

pitch black [piʧ blǽk] a. 칠흑같이 어두운, 새까만
If a place or the night is pitch black, it is completely dark.

barrel [bǽrəl] v. 쏜살같이 질주하다
If a vehicle or person is barrelling in a particular direction, they are moving very quickly in that direction.

source [sɔːrs] n. 원천, 근원
A source is where something comes from.

blaze [bleiz] v. 활활 타다
When a fire blazes, it burns strongly and brightly.

passenger [pǽsəndʒər] n. 승객
A passenger in a vehicle such as a bus, boat, or plane is a person who is traveling in it, but who is not driving it or working on it.

hover [hʌ́vər] v. 맴돌다
To hover means to stay in the same position in the air without moving forward or backward.

puzzled [pʌzld] a. 어리둥절해하는
Someone who is puzzled is confused because they do not understand something.

burst [bəːrst] v. (burst-burst) 불쑥 움직이다
To burst into or out of a place means to enter or leave it suddenly with a lot of energy or force.

flood [flʌd] v. 가득 들어오다
If light floods a place or floods into it, it suddenly fills it.

reflection [riflékʃən] n. (거울 등에 비친) 모습
A reflection is an image that you can see in a mirror or in glass or water.

flicker [flíkər] v. (불·빛 등이) 깜박거리다; 스치다
If a light or flame flickers, it shines unsteadily.

ticket [tíkit] n. (벌금을 부과하는) 딱지
A ticket is an official piece of paper which orders you to pay a fine or to appear in court because you have committed a driving or parking offence.

shut down idiom (공장·가게의) 문을 닫다
If a factory or business shuts down or if someone shuts it down, work there stops or it no longer trades as a business.

city hall [siti hɔ́ːl] n. 시청
A city hall refers to the building that houses the administrative offices of a city.

whirl [hwəːrl] v. 빙빙 돌다
When you whirl, you turn or spin around rapidly.

whip [hwip] v. 휙 빼내다
If someone whips something out or whips it off, they take it out or take it off very quickly and suddenly.

dodge [dadʒ] v. (몸을) 피하다, 비키다
If you dodge something, you avoid it by quickly moving aside or out of reach so that it cannot hit or reach you.

apologize [əpálədʒàiz] v. 사과하다
To apologize means to express regret for something wrong that one has done.

stream [striːm] v. 흘러가다
If a liquid streams somewhere, it flows or comes out in large amounts.

struggle [strʌgl] v. 노력하다, 애쓰다
If you struggle to do something, you try hard to do it, even though other people or things may be making it difficult for you to succeed.

mutter [mʌ́tər] v. 중얼거리다
If you mutter, you speak very quietly so that you cannot easily be heard, often because you are complaining about something.

collide [kəláid] v. 부딪치다
If someone or something collides with another person or thing, they crash into them.

float [flout] v. (물 위나 공중에서) 떠다니다, 흘러가다
Something that floats in or through the air hangs in it or moves slowly and gently through it.

reform [rifɔ́ːrm] v. 형태를 다시 잡다
To reform means to change the shape of or to make changes to something.

drift [drift] v. 떠다니다
When something drifts somewhere, it is carried there by the movement of wind or water.

nursery school [nɔ́ːrsəri school] n. 유치원
A nursery school or a nursery is a school for very young children.

block [blak] v. 막다, 차단하다
If you block someone's way, you prevent them from going somewhere or entering a place by standing in front of them.

balloon [bəlúːn] n. 열기구 풍선
A balloon is a large bag made of strong material that is filled with hot air or gas to make it rise in the air, usually carrying a basket for passengers.

amazed [əméizd] a. 놀란
If you are amazed, you are very surprised.

tumble [tʌmbl] v. 굴러 떨어지다
If someone or something tumbles somewhere, they fall there with a rolling or bouncing movement.

land [lænd] v. (땅·표면에) 떨어지다
When someone or something lands, they come down to the ground after moving through the air or falling.

sharp [ʃaːrp] a. 급격한
A sharp bend or turn is one that changes direction suddenly.

skid [skid] v. 미끄러지다
If a person skids, it slides, usually sideways, especially on slippery ground.

slip [slip] v. 슬며시 가다
If you slip somewhere, you go there quickly and quietly.

shimmy [ʃími] v. 움직이다
To shimmy means to move or shake your body from side to side.

work one's way idiom 노력하며 나아가다
If you work your way through a place, you move out of a particular position slowly or with difficulty.

passageway [pǽsidʒwèi] n. 통로
A passageway is a narrow area, like a hallway, that connects one place to another.

opening [óupəniŋ] n. 구멍, 통로
An opening is a hole or empty space through which things or people can pass.

crevice [krévis] n. (바위나 담에 생긴) 틈
A crevice is a narrow crack or a gap, especially in a rock or a wall.

grunt [grʌnt] v. 끙 앓는 소리를 내다
If you grunt, you make a low sound, especially because you are annoyed or not interested in something.

emerge [imə́:rdʒ] v. 나타나다
To emerge means to come out from somewhere and become possible to see.

swipe [swaip] v. 훔치다
If you swipe something, you steal it quickly.

chili [ʧíli] n. 고추, 칠리
Chilies are small red or green peppers.

vendor [véndər] n. 상인
A vendor is someone who sells things from a small stall or cart.

squirt [skwə́:rt] v. 찍 뿌리다
If you squirt a liquid somewhere, the liquid comes out of a narrow opening in a thin fast stream.

disappointing [dìsəpɔ́intiŋ] a. 실망스러운
Something that is disappointing is not as good or as large as you hoped it would be.

nearby [nìərbái] a. 바로 가까이의
If something is nearby, it is only a short distance away.

grate [greit] n. (창·배수구 따위의) 격자
A grate is a frame of metal bars over the opening to a drain in the ground.

spout [spaut] v. 뿜어져 나오다
If someone spouts up, they come out of something like a stream with great force.

revolving door [riválviŋ dɔ́:r] n. 회전문
A revolving door is a type of door in an entrance to a large building that turns around in a circle as people go through it.

dim [dim] v. 희미해지다
If a light dims, it becomes less bright.

despair [dispéər] n. 절망
Despair is the feeling that everything is wrong and that nothing will improve.

holler [hálər] v. 소리지르다, 고함치다
If you holler, you shout loudly.

slump [slʌmp] v. 구부정해지다
If your shoulders or head slump or are slumped, they bend forward because you are unhappy, tired, or unconscious.

inner [ínər] a. 내부의
Inner is used to describe something that is inside or contained within something else.

prismatic [prizmǽtik] a. 선명한
If something is prismatic, it is very bright and clear.

glow [glou] v. 빛나다
When something glows, it produces a steady light.

weary [wíəri] a. 지친
If you are weary, you are really tired, like after a long day of playing or not getting enough sleep.

canister [kǽnəstər] n. 통, 용기
A canister is a metal, plastic, or china container with a lid.

load [loud] v. 싣다
If you load a vehicle or a container, you put a large quantity of things into it.

vacuum [vǽkjuəm] n. 진공
A vacuum is a space that contains no air or other gas.

let go idiom (손으로 잡고 있던 것을) 놓다
If you let something go, it means you stop holding it.

fleck [flek] n. 얼룩
A fleck is a tiny spot or mark, sometimes with color.

take over idiom ~을 이어받다
If you take over a company, you get control of it.

murmur [mə́:rmə] v. 중얼거리다
If you murmur something, you say it very quietly so that not many people can hear what you are saying.

chest [ʧest] n. 가슴
Your chest is the top part of the front of your body where your ribs, lungs, and heart are.

shield [ʃi:ld] n. 보호막, 방패
Something which is a shield against a particular danger or risk provides protection from it.

tear [tɛər] v. 찢다
If you tear paper, cloth, or another material, or if it tears, you pull it into two pieces or you pull it so that a hole appears in it.

processing [prásesiŋ] n. 처리
Processing means the act of dealing officially with a document or request.

department [dipá:rtmənt] n. 부서
A department is one of the sections in an organization such as a government, business, or university.

gesture [dʒésʧər] v. 가리키다, 몸짓을 하다
If you gesture, you use movements of your hands or head in order to tell someone something or draw their attention to something.

growl [graul] v. 으르렁거리듯 말하다
If someone growls something, they say something in a low, rough, and angry voice.

frustration [frʌstréiʃən] n. 좌절감
Frustration is a feeling you get when you can't do or get what you want.

plead [pli:d] v. 변호하다, 진술하다
If you plead the case or cause of someone or something, you speak out in their support or defence.

perk up idiom 기운을 차리다
If something perks you up or if you perk up, you become cheerful and lively, after feeling tired, bored, or depressed.

Check Your Reading Speed

1분에 몇 단어를 읽는지 리딩 속도를 측정해 보세요.

$$\frac{1{,}295 \text{ words}}{\text{reading time (\ \ ) sec}} \times 60 = (\quad) \text{ WPM}$$

Build Your Vocabulary

tangled [tǽŋgld] a. 뒤얽힌
When vines or other things are tangled, they are mixed up together in an untidy way.

leafy [líːfi] a. 잎이 많은
Leafy describes something that has many leaves or is covered with leaves.

vine [vain] n. 덩굴 식물
A vine is a plant that grows up or over things, especially one which produces grapes.

barely [béərli] ad. 가까스로
You use barely to say that something is only just true or only just the case.

thick [θik] a. (나무 등이) 빽빽한, 울창한
If something that consists of several things is thick, it has a large number of them very close together.

stalk [stɔːk] n. (식물의) 줄기
A stalk is a long narrow part of a plant that supports leaves, fruits, or flowers.

branch [brænʧ] n. 나뭇가지
A branch is a part of a tree that grows out from the trunk and on which leaves, flowers, and fruit grow.

snap [snæp] v. 휙 움직이다; 날카롭게 말하다
If you snap something into a particular position, or if it snaps into that position, it moves quickly into that position, with a sharp sound.

duck [dʌk] v. 휙 수그리다
If you duck, you move your head or the top half of your body quickly downward to avoid something that might hit you, or to avoid being seen.

earth [əːrθ] n. 흙
Earth is the substance in which plants grow that covers most of the land.

cluttered [klʌ́tərd] a. 어수선한
If a place is cluttered, filled with more items than it needs or can easily hold, making it hard to use or move around in.

nameplate [néimplèit] n. 명찰, 명패
A nameplate is a piece of metal, wood, or plastic which has a person's name written on it.

overgrown [òuvərgróun] a. 마구 자란
When grass or plants are overgrown, they have grown in an uncontrolled way.

sprout [spraut] v. 돋아나다, 자라다
When leaves, shoots, or plants sprout somewhere, they grow there.

grassy [grǽsi] a. 풀이 무성한
If something is grassy, it means it is covered with a lot of soft green plants.

mustache [mʌ́stæʃ] n. 콧수염
A mustache is the hair growing on the upper lip somone's face.

tidy [táidi] a. 깔끔한
Something that is tidy is neat and is arranged in an organized way.

trim [trim] v. 다듬다
To trim something means to make it neat by cutting it slightly.

mumble [mʌ́mbl] v. 중얼거리다
To mumble means to speak quietly and unclearly.

tree-stump [trí:-stʌmp] n. 그루터기, 베어낸 나무 뿌리
A tree-stump is the small part of a tree that is left after the rest has been cut down.

inbox [ínbàks] n. 미결 서류함
An inbox is a shallow container used in offices to put letters and documents in before they are dealt with.

overflow [òuvərflóu] v. 넘치다
If a place or container is overflowing with people or things, it is too full of them.

vacuum [vǽkjuəm] n. 진공
A vacuum is a space that contains no air or other gas.

nervously [nə́:rvəsli] ad. 초조하게
If you do something nervously, you do it while feeling worried or not relaxed.

citation [saitéiʃən] n. 위반 딱지
A citation is an official order for someone to appear in court or pay a fine for doing something illegal.

canister [kǽnəstər] n. 통, 용기
A canister is a metal, plastic, or china container with a lid.

rot [rat] n. 썩음, 부패
If there is rot in something, especially something that is made of wood, parts of it have decayed and fallen apart.

hesitate [hézətèit] v. 망설이다, 주저하다
If you hesitate, you do not speak or act for a short time, usually because you are uncertain, embarrassed, or worried about what you are going to say or do.

have a word idiom 잠깐 이야기를 하다
If you have a word with someone, you have a short conversation with them.

nod [nad] v. (고개를) 끄덕이다
If you nod, you move your head up and down to show agreement, understanding, or approval.

lean [liːn] v. (몸을) 숙이다
When you lean in a particular direction, you bend your body in that direction.

hiss [his] n. 쉬익 하는 소리
A hiss is a sound like a long 's'.

singe [sindʒ] v. 그슬리다
If you singe something, you burn it slightly on the surface.

handprint [hǽndprint] n. 손자국
A handprint is a mark left by the hand.

stare [stɛər] v. 빤히 쳐다보다
If you stare at someone or something, you look at them for a long time.

unamused [ʌnəmjuːzd] a. 못마땅해하는
If you are unamused, you feel somewhat annoyed or disapproving.

breezy [bríːzi] a. 쾌활한
If you describe someone as breezy, you mean that they behave in a casual, cheerful, and confident manner.

permit [pərmít] v. 허용하다; n. 허가증; 허가
If someone permits something, they allow it to happen, especially by an official decision, rule, or law.

wink [wiŋk] v. 윙크하다
When you wink at someone, you look toward them and close one eye very briefly, usually as a signal that something is a joke or a secret.

skate around idiom 언급을 피하다
If you skate around an action, you avoid doing it because it is something difficult to do.

guilty [gílti] a. 유죄의
If someone is guilty of doing something wrong, they have done that thing.

crack a smile idiom 미소 짓다
To crack a smile means to begin smiling.

realize [ríːəlàiz] v. 인식하다, 자각하다
If you realize something, you become aware of it, understand it, or accept it after thinking about it or discovering it.

out loud idiom 소리내어
If you say something out loud, you say it so that other people can hear you.

exact [igzǽkt] a. 정확한
If something is exact, it means it's just right, with no mistakes.

let down idiom ~을 실망시키다
If you let someone down, you disappoint them, by not doing something that you have said you will do or that they expected you to do.

flare [flɛər] v. 확 타오르다
When a fire flares up, it suddenly burns more intensely.

personal [pə́rsənl] a. 개인적인
If something is personal, it's connected with a person's private life, rather than their job or official position.

get to idiom ~을 감동시키다
When something gets to you, your emotions are stirred.

stuff [stʌf] v. 쑤셔 넣다
If you stuff something somewhere, you push it there quickly and roughly.

disappointed [dìsəpɔ́intid] a. 실망한, 낙담한
If you are disappointed, you are rather sad because something has not happened or because something is not as good as you had hoped.

grab [græb] v. 움켜잡다
If you grab something, you take it or pick it up suddenly and roughly.

shove [ʃʌv] v. 아무렇게나 넣다
If you shove something somewhere, you push it there quickly and carelessly.

suspend [səspénd] v. 떠 있다
If something is suspended in something else, it floats in liquid or air without moving.

take a breath idiom 심호흡을 하다
If you say that you took a breath before doing something dangerous or frightening, you mean that you tried to make yourself feel strong and confident.

knock [nak] v. (움직이도록) 치다
If you knock something, you touch or hit it roughly, especially so that it falls or moves.

eke out idiom 힘겹게 해내다
To eke out is to get by with difficulty or a struggle.

ashamed [əʃéimd] a. 수치스러운
If someone is ashamed, they feel embarrassed or guilty because of something they have done.

retire [ritáiər] v. 은퇴하다
When people retire, they leave their job and usually stop working completely.

weep [wi:p] v. 울다
If someone weeps, they cry.

hang on one's every word idiom ~의 말을 귀 기울여 듣다
If you hang on someone's every word, you listen very carefully to what they are saying.

explode [iksplóud] v. 폭발하다
If an object such as a bomb explodes or if someone or something explodes it, it bursts loudly and with great force, often causing damage or injury.

roar [rɔ:r] v. 고함치다
If someone roars, they shout something in a very loud voice.

clear [kliər] v. (연기 등이) 걷히다
When fog or mist clears, it slowly disappears.

rimmed [rímd] a. ~의 테가 있는
If something is rimmed with a substance or color, it has that substance or color around its border.

askew [əskjú:] ad. 비스듬히
When something is askew, it is not straight or not level with what it should be level with.

burn to a crisp idiom 새까맣게 타다
If something burns to a crisp, it becomes completely burnt.

douse [daus] v. (불을) 끄다
If you douse a fire, you stop it burning by pouring a lot of water over it.

flaming [fléimiŋ] a. 불타는
Flaming describes something that is burning or on fire.

scorched [skɔ:rʧt] a. 그을은
If something is scorched, it has been burned on the surface.

flatly [flǽtli] ad. 심드렁하게
If you say something flatly, you say it in a way that shows very little interest or emotion.

beg [beg] v. 애원하다, 간청하다
If you beg someone to do something, you ask them very anxiously or eagerly to do it.

desperation [dèspəréiʃən] n. 절망감
Desperation is the feeling that you have when you are in such a bad situation that you will try anything to change it.

brochure [brouʃúər] n. (안내용) 책자
A brochure is a magazine or thin book with pictures that gives you information about a product or service.

sigh [sai] v. 한숨을 쉬다
When you sigh, you let out a deep breath, as a way of expressing feelings such as disappointment, tiredness, or pleasure.

absolutely [æbsəlú:tli] ad. 극도로
If you feel something absolutely, you feel that way to the highest degree.

utterly [ʌ́tərli] ad. 완전히
You use utterly to emphasize that something is very great in extent, degree, or amount.

defeated [difíːtid] a. 좌절한
If you are defeated, you are sad and unable to deal with problems.

teary [tíəri] a. 눈물이 글썽한
When your eyes are teary, they are moist or shiny as if you are about to cry.

cough [kɔːf] v. 기침하다
When you cough, you force air out of your throat with a sudden, harsh noise.

burst [bəːrst] v. 터지다, 파열하다
If something bursts or if you burst it, it suddenly breaks open or splits open and the air
or other substance inside it comes out.

leak [liːk] v. (액체·기체가) 새다
If a liquid or gas leaks, it escapes through a hole or crack.

desperately [déspərətli] ad. 필사적으로
If you do something desperately, you do it in a way that shows you must do something
to change it.

mess [mes] n. 엉망인 상태
If you say that something is a mess or in a mess, you think that it is in an untidy state.

ruin [rúːin] v. 망치다
To ruin something means to severely harm, damage, or spoil it.

wince [wins] v. 움찔하고 놀라다
When you wince, the muscles of your face tighten suddenly because you have felt a
pain or have seen something unpleasant.

guilt [gilt] n. 죄책감
Guilt is an unhappy feeling that you have because you have done something wrong or
think that you have done something wrong.

chase [ʧeis] v. 뒤쫓다
If you chase after someone, you run or move quickly to catch up to them.

drip [drip] v. 떨어지다
When liquid drips somewhere, or you drip it somewhere, it falls in individual small
drops.

cringe [krindʒ] v. 움찔하다
If you cringe at something, you feel embarrassed or disgusted, and perhaps show this
feeling in your expression or by making a slight movement.

sting [stiŋ] n. 따가움
If you feel a sting, you feel a sharp pain in your skin or other part of your body.

fib [fib] v. 거짓말을 하다
If someone is fibbing, they are telling lies.

spit [spit] v. (spat/spit-spat/spit) 내뱉듯이 말하다
If someone spits an insult or comment, they say it in an angry or hostile way.

water down idiom ~을 약화시키다
If you water down something, you make it less effective or powerful.

grumble [grʌmbl] v. 투덜거리다
If someone grumbles, they complain about something in a bad-tempered way.

violently [váiələntli] ad. 격렬하게
If something happens violently, it happens with a lot of force or energy.

rub [rʌb] v. 쓰다듬다
If you rub a part of your body, you move your hand or fingers backward and forward over it while pressing firmly.

get through idiom (곤란 등을) 벗어나다
To get through something means to to manage to deal with a difficult situation or to stay alive until it is over.

sink [siŋk] v. (sank-sunk) 주저앉다
If you sink, you move into a lower position, for example by sitting down in a chair or kneeling.

include [inklú:d] v. 포함하다
If one thing includes another thing, it has the other thing as one of its parts.

pregnant [prégnənt] a. 임신한
If a woman or a female animal is pregnant, she has a baby or babies developing in her body.

grave [greiv] a. 엄숙한
When someone's voice is grave, they are being serious and often worried.

brew [bru:] v. (폭풍우 등이) 일어나려고 하다
If a storm is brewing, large clouds are beginning to form and the sky is becoming dark because there is going to be a storm.

rooftop [rúftàp] n. 지붕, 옥상
A rooftop is the outside part of the roof of a building.

ferocious [fəróuʃəs] a. 맹렬한
If something is ferocious, it is very violent or strong.

debris [dəbríː] n. 파편
Debris is pieces from something that has been destroyed or pieces of rubbish or unwanted material that are spread around.

crash [kræʃ] v. 부딪치다, 박살나다
If something crashes somewhere, it moves and hits something else violently, making a loud noise.

cauldron [kɔ́ːldrən] n. 솥, 큰 냄비
A cauldron is a very large, round metal pot used for cooking over a fire.

capture [kǽpʧər] v. 담다
If you capture something, you succeed in getting or holding them.

collapse [kəlǽps] v. 붕괴되다
If a building or other structure collapses, it falls down very suddenly.

pile [pail] n. 더미
A pile of things is a mass of them that is high in the middle and has sloping sides.

rubble [rʌbl] n. 돌무더기, 잔해
When a building is destroyed, the pieces of brick, stone, or other materials that remain are referred to as rubble.

damage [dǽmidʒ] v. 손상을 주다, 훼손하다
To damage an object means to break it, spoil it physically, or stop it from working properly.

shore [ʃɔːr] n. 해안가
The shore is the land along the edge of a sea, lake, or wide river.

mop [map] v. 대걸레로 닦다
If you mop a surface such as a floor, you clean it with a piece of equipment for washing floors.

emotional [imóuʃənl] a. 감정적인
If someone is or becomes emotional, they show their feelings very openly, especially because they are upset.

reignite [riːignáit] v. 재점화되다
To reignite means to start burning again.

vow [vau] v. 맹세하다
If you vow to do something, you make a serious promise or decision that you will do it.

cheek [ʧiːk] n. 뺨, 볼
Your cheeks are the sides of your face below your eyes.

wearily [wíərili] ad. 피곤한 듯이
When you do something wearily, it means you're doing it while feeling tired or without much energy.

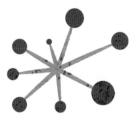

7 & 8

1. Why did Ember want to talk to Gale?

    A. To know more about Gale

    B. To get tickets for the game

    C. To cancel the tickets Wade had written

    D. To ask questions about airball

2. Why was Lutz not playing well?

    A. Because he didn't like the game

    B. Because his mom was sick

    C. Because he was tired

    D. Because he was scared

3. What did the crowd do after Wade started supporting Lutz?

    A. They joined in the chant.

    B. They left the game.

    C. They started booing.

    D. They all became quiet.

4. Why was the water problem in Ember's shop surprising?

    A. Water was needed there.

    B. Wade is scared of water.

    C. Ember knew the source of the water.

    D. There should have been no water there.

5. What caused Wade to end up in Ember's shop?

    A. He dived into the hole of the pipe.

    B. He got sucked into a pipe.

    C. He was invited by Ember.

    D. He wrote tickets for Fire people.

Check Your Reading Speed

1분에 몇 단어를 읽는지 리딩 속도를 측정해 보세요.

$$\frac{1,343 \text{ words}}{\text{reading time (\quad) sec}} \times 60 = (\quad) \text{ WPM}$$

Build Your Vocabulary

head [hed] v. (특정 방향으로) 가다
If you are heading for a particular place, you are going toward that place.

city hall [síti hɔ́:l] n. 시청
A city hall refers to the building that houses the administrative offices of a city.

vibrate [váibreit] v. 흔들리다
When something vibrates, it shakes repeatedly and quickly, often felt as rhythmic movement.

approach [əpróuʧ] v. 다가가다, 접근하다
To approach something means to get closer to it.

department [dipá:rtmənt] n. 부서
A department is one of the sections in an organization such as a government, business, or university.

flame [fleim] n. 불꽃
A flame is the hot, bright, and burning gas produced by something on fire.

glance [glæns] v. 흘낏 보다
If you glance at something or someone, you look at them very quickly and then look away again immediately.

desperately [déspərətli] ad. 필사적으로
If you do something desperately, you do it in a way that shows you must do something to change it.

pat [pæt] v. 가볍게 치다
If you pat something or someone, you tap them lightly, usually with your hand held flat.

stomp [stamp] v. 발을 구르다
If you stomp on something, you put your foot down on the it hard and quickly.

smolder [smóuldər] v. (서서히) 타다
If something smolders, it burns slowly, producing smoke but not flames.

eyebrow [áibràu] n. 눈썹
Your eyebrows are the lines of hair which grow above your eyes.

embarrassment [imbǽrəsmənt] n. 당황스러움, 난처함
Embarrassment is a feeling of being shy, ashamed, or guilty about something.

boss [bɔːs] n. 상사
A boss is someone who is in charge and can give orders to others.

settle [setl] v. 편하게 앉다
If you settle yourself somewhere or settle somewhere, you sit down or make yourself comfortable.

pump [pʌmp] v. 흔들다, 움직이다
To pump means to move something very quickly in and out or up and down.

fist [fist] n. 주먹
Your hand is referred to as your fist when you have bent your fingers in toward the palm in order to hit someone, to make an angry gesture, or to hold something.

frustration [frʌstréiʃən] n. 좌절감
Frustration is a feeling you get when you can't do or get what you want.

come by idiom 잠깐 들르다
If you come by somewhere, you make a short visit to a place on your way to somewhere else.

pass [pæs] n. 무료 입장권
A pass is something like a ticket that allows you to enter or go to a specific place.

perk up idiom 기운을 차리다
If something perks you up or if you perk up, you become cheerful and lively, after feeling tired, bored, or depressed.

plural [plúərəl] a. 두 가지 이상의
Plural means relating to more than one.

look up idiom 나아지다
If a situation is looking up, it is improving.

district [dístrikt] n. 구역
A district is a particular area of a town or country.

awe [ɔ:] n. 경외감
Awe is the feeling of respect and amazement that you have when you are faced with something wonderful and often rather frightening.

throng [θrɔ:ŋ] n. 인파, 군중
A throng is a large crowd of people.

stadium [stéidiəm] n. 경기장
A stadium is a large sports ground with rows of seats all round it.

cylindrical [silíndrikəl] a. 원통형의
If something is cylindrical, it is shaped like a long, straight piece with round sides and two flat ends.

marquee [ma:rkí:] n. 대형 천막
A marquee is a large sign over a building that indicates the information about what is happening inside the builing.

make one's way idiom 나아가다
When you make your way somewhere, you walk or travel there.

stand [stænd] n. 관중석
A stand at a sports ground is a large structure where people sit or stand to watch what is happening.

fluffy [flʌfi] a. 솜털 같은
If something is fluffly, it looks as if it is soft and light.

hoop [hu:p] n. (농구의) 링
A hoop is the ring that players try to throw the ball into in order to score points for their team.

scan [skæn] v. (유심히) 살피다
When you scan a place or a group of people, you look at it carefully, usually because you are looking for something or someone.

swell [swel] v. 부풀다
If the amount or size of something swells or if something swells it, it becomes larger than it was before.

bellow [bélou] v. 고함치다
To bellow means to shout in a deep, loud voice.

flicker [flíkər] v. 스치다; 깜빡거리다
If an emotion or expression flickers on someone's face or through their mind, it exists or is shown for only a short time.

chest [ʧest] n. 가슴
Your chest is the top part of the front of your body where your ribs, lungs, and heart are.

vendor [véndər] n. 상인
A vendor is someone who sells things from a small stall or cart.

row [rou] n. 열, 줄
A row of things or people is a number of them arranged in a line.

encourage [inkɔ́:ridʒ] v. 격려하다
If you encourage someone, you give them confidence, for example by letting them know that what they are doing is good and telling them that they should continue to do it.

suck [sʌk] v. (액체·공기 등을) 빨아들이다
If something sucks a liquid, gas, or object in a particular direction, it draws it there with a powerful force.

greet [gri:t] v. 인사하다, 맞이하다
To greet someone means to say hello to them or to welcome them.

thunder [θʌ́ndər] v. 고함치다
If you thunder something, you say it loudly and forcefully, especially because you are angry.

score [skɔ:r] n. 득점; v. 득점하다
The score in a game is the result of it or the current situation, as indicated by the number of goals, runs, or points obtained by the two teams or players.

rumble [rʌ́mbl] v. 우르릉거리는 소리를 내다
If someone or something rumbles, it makes a low, continuous noise.

blast [blæst] v. 맹비난하다
To blast someone or something means to criticize them strongly.

courage [kɔ́:ridʒ] n. 용기
Courage is the quality shown by someone who decides to do something difficult or dangerous, even though they may be afraid.

bunch [bʌnʧ] n. 다발, 묶음
A bunch of things is a number of things, especially a large number.

ticket [tíkit] n. (벌금을 부과하는) 딱지
A ticket is an official piece of paper which orders you to pay a fine or to appear in court because you have committed a driving or parking offence.

call [kɔːl] n. (심판의) 판정
A call is the decision made by a referee in a sports game.

impatiently [impéiʃəntli] ad. 참지 못하고
If you do something impatiently, you do it in a way that shows you are annoyed, especially because you have to wait for a long time.

citation [saitéiʃən] n. 위반 딱지
A citation is an official order for someone to appear in court or pay a fine for doing something illegal.

shoot [ʃuːt] v. (shot-shot) (눈길 등을) 휙 던지다; 휙 움직이다
If you shoot a look at someone, you look at them quickly and briefly, often in a way that expresses your feelings.

shrug [ʃrʌg] v. (어깨를) 으쓱하다
If you shrug, you raise your shoulders and then drop them to show that you do not know or care about something.

work out idiom ~을 해결하다
If you work out a solution to a problem or mystery, you manage to find the solution by thinking or talking about it.

rotate [róuteit] v. 회전하다
When something rotates or when you rotate it, it turns with a circular movement.

puffy [pʌ́fi] a. 뭉게뭉게 피어 오른
If something is puffy, it is soft and light.

glare [glɛər] v. 노려보다
When you glare at someone, you look at them with an angry expression on your face.

boo [buː] v. 야유하다
To boo means to shout 'boo' or make other loud sounds to indicate that you do not like them or their performance.

darken [dáːrkən] v. 어두워지다
If something darkens or if a person or thing darkens it, it becomes darker.

bummer [bʌ́mər] n. 실망(스러운 일)
If you say that something is a bummer, you mean that it is unpleasant or annoying.

whirl [hwəːrl] v. 빙빙 돌다
When you whirl, you turn or spin around rapidly.

repeat [ripíːt] v. 한 번 더 말하다
If you repeat something, you say or write it again.

block [blak] v. (시야를) 가리다, 차단하다
If something blocks your view, it prevents you from seeing something because it is between you and that thing.

flash [flæʃ] v. 번쩍이다
If a light flashes or if you flash a light, it shines with a sudden bright light, especially as quick, regular flashes of light.

sob [sab] a. 눈물 나게 하는
A sob story is a story that someone tells you just to make you feel sorry for them.

streak [striːk] v. 기다란 자국을 내다, 줄무늬를 넣다
If something streaks a surface, it makes long stripes or marks on the surface.

ominously [ámənəsli] ad. 불길하게
If something happens ominously, it is done in a way that makes you think something bad will happen.

way [wei] ad. 훨씬
You can use way to emphasize, for example, that something is a great distance away or is very much below or above a particular level or amount.

overpaid [òuvərpéid] a. 과다한 보수를 받는
If you say that someone is overpaid, you mean that you think they are paid more than they deserve for the work they do.

puff [pʌf] n. 불룩한 것
A puff of something such as air or smoke is a small amount of it that is blown out from somewhere.

loom [luːm] v. 어렴풋이 나타나다
If something looms over you, it appears as a large or unclear shape, often in a frightening way.

dare [dɛər] v. 해 보라고 하다, 부추기다
If you dare someone to do something, you challenge them to prove that they are not frightened of doing it.

furious [fjúəriəs] a. 몹시 화가 난
Someone who is furious is extremely angry.

reform [rifɔ́ːrm] v. 형태를 다시 잡다
To reform means to change the shape of or to make changes to something.

gasp [gæsp] v. 헉 하고 숨을 쉬다
When you gasp, you take a short quick breath through your mouth, especially when you are surprised or shocked.

race [reis] v. 급히 가다
If you race somewhere, you go there as quickly as possible.

guard [gaːrd] v. 지키다, 보호하다
If you guard a place, person, or object, you stand near them in order to watch and protect them.

spirit [spírit] n. 기백, 기상, 활기
Spirit is the liveliness and energy that someone shows in what they do.

sink [siŋk] v. (sank-sunk) 낙담하다
If your heart or your spirits sink, you become depressed or lose hope.

funk [fʌŋk] n. 낙담, 의기소침
If someone is in a funk, they are sad, especially because they are in a situation they cannot control.

prove [pruːv] v. 입증하다, 증명하다
If you prove that something is true, you show by means of argument or evidence that it is definitely true.

opponent [əpóunənt] n. 상대
In a sporting contest, your opponent is the person who is playing against you.

agitated [ǽdʒitèitid] a. 흥분한
If someone is agitated, they are very worried or upset, and show this in their behavior, movements, or voice.

survey [sərvéi] v. 살피다
If you survey something, you look at or consider the whole of it carefully.

skyward [skáiwərd] ad. 하늘을 향해
If you look skyward, you look up toward the sky.

chant [ʧænt] n. 구호
A chant is a word or group of words that is repeated over and over again.

cheer [ʧiər] v. 환호하다
When people cheer, they shout loudly to show their approval or to encourage someone who is doing something such as taking part in a game.

section [sékʃən] n. 구역
A section of something is one of the parts into which it is divided or from which it is formed.

pick up idiom (습관·재주 등을) 들이게[익히게] 되다
If you pick up something such as a skill or an idea, you acquire it without effort over a period of time.

ripple [ripl] v. 잔물결을 일으키다
When the surface of an area of water ripples or when something ripples it, a number of little waves appear on it.

follow suit idiom 방금 남이 한 대로 따라 하다
If people follow suit, they do the same thing that someone else has just done.

shield [ʃiːld] v. 보호하다, 가리다
When you shield something, you protect it from harm or danger.

energize [énərdʒàiz] v. 기운을 북돋우다
To energize someone means to give them the enthusiasm and determination to do something.

slam [slæm] v. 세게 놓다
If you slam something down, you put it there quickly and with great force.

leap [liːp] v. (서둘러) ~하다
If you leap somewhere, you move there suddenly and quickly.

way to go idiom 잘했어!
You can say 'way to go' to someone to tell that they have done something well, or that you are proud of their achievement.

inspire [inspáiər] v. 고무하다, 격려하다
If someone or something inspires you to do something new or unusual, they make you want to do it.

tide [taid] n. 흐름
The tide of opinion, for example, is what the majority of people think at a particular time.

slap [slæp] v. 철썩 때리다
To slap means to hit quickly and with a flat hand.

palm [pa:m] n. 손바닥
The palm of your hand is the inside part of your hand, between your fingers and your wrist.

awful [ɔ́:fəl] a. 끔찍한
If you say that something is awful, you think that they are not very good.

lower [lóuər] v. 내리다, 낮추다
If you lower something, you move it slowly downward.

awkward [ɔ́:kwərd] a. 어색한
An awkward movement or position is uncomfortable or clumsy.

smack [smæk] n. 탁 (하는 소리)
A smack is a short loud sound made when something hits a surface.

Check Your Reading Speed
1분에 몇 단어를 읽는지 리딩 속도를 측정해 보세요.

$$\frac{893 \text{ words}}{\text{reading time ( ) sec}} \times 60 = (\quad) \text{ WPM}$$

Build Your Vocabulary

rowdy [ráudi] a. 소란스러운
When people are rowdy, they are noisy and behave in a way that may cause trouble.

pour [pɔːr] v. 쏟아져 나오다
If people pour into or out of a place, they go there quickly and in large numbers.

stadium [stéidiəm] n. 경기장
A stadium is a large sports ground with rows of seats all round it.

pound [paund] v. (음악 소리가) 쿵쾅거리다
If music is pounding out, it is playing loudly.

head to toe idiom 머리에서 발끝까지
Head to toe means all over your body.

gear [giər] n. 복장
Gear is the clothes for a particular occasion.

grin [grin] v. 활짝 웃다
When you grin, you smile broadly.

admit [ædmít] v. 인정하다
If you admit something, you agree, often unwillingly, that it is true.

churn [ʧəːrn] v. 당황하게 하다, 자제를 잃게 하다
If you are churned up, you can feel upset or angry.

puff [pʌf] n. 불룩한 것
A puff of something such as air or smoke is a small amount of it that is blown out from somewhere.

take over idiom ~을 이어받다
If you take over a company, you get control of it.

out loud idiom 소리 내어
If you say something out loud, you say it so that other people can hear you.

let down idiom ~을 실망시키다
If you let someone down, you disappoint them, by not doing something that you have said you will do or that they expected you to do.

let down one's guard idiom 경계를 늦추다
If you let your guard down, you relax when you should be careful and alert, often with unpleasant consequences.

confused [kənfjúːzd] a. 혼란스러워하는
If you are confused, you do not know what to think or what to do.

shut off idiom (가스·수돗물 등을) 차단하다
If you shut off a supply of gas or water, you stop it from flowing or reaching a place.

ticket [tíkit] n. (벌금을 부과하는) 딱지
A ticket is an official piece of paper which orders you to pay a fine or to appear in court because you have committed a driving or parking offence.

take apart idiom 분해하다
If you take something apart, you separate it into the different parts that it is made of.

figure out idiom 알아내다
If you figure out a solution to a problem or the reason for something, you succeed in solving it or understanding it.

bet [bet] v. (~이) 틀림없다
You use expressions such as 'I bet,' 'I'll bet,' and 'you can bet' to indicate that you are sure something is true.

fluff [flʌf] v. 망치다
If you fluff something that you are trying to do, you are unsuccessful or you do it badly.

track down idiom ~을 찾아내다
If you track down someone or something, you find them, or find information about them, after a difficult or long search.

canal [kənal] n. 운하
A canal is a long, narrow stretch of water that has been made for boats to travel along or to bring water to a particular area.

track [træk] v. 추적하다
If you track someone or something, you investigate them, because you are interested in finding out more about them.

source [sɔːrs] n. 원천, 근원
A source is where something comes from.

intrigued [intríːgd] a. 아주 흥미로워하는
If you are intrigued, you are very interested in something and wanting to know more about it.

crew [kruː] n. (함께 일을 하는) 조, 반
A crew is a group of people with special technical skills who work together on a task or project.

jump on board idiom (단체·활동 등에) 참가하다
If you jump on board, you join a group or activity, especially one that has been operating or functioning for some time.

hopeful [hóupfəl] a. 희망을 품은, 기대에 부푼
A hopeful action is one that you do in the hope that you will get what you want to get.

cut off idiom (말을) 중단시키다
If you cut someone off, you interrupt them when they are speaking.

shut down idiom (공장·가게의) 문을 닫다
If a factory or business shuts down or if someone shuts it down, work there stops or it no longer trades as a business.

drift [drift] v. 떠다니다
When something drifts somewhere, it is carried there by the movement of wind or water.

way [wei] ad. 훨씬
You can use way to emphasize, for example, that something is a great distance away or is very much below or above a particular level or amount.

plunk [plʌŋk] v. 털썩 하고 놓다
If you plunk something somewhere, you put it there without great care.

instantly [ínstəntli] ad. 즉시
If something happens instantly, it happens at once.

element [éləmənt] n. 원소
An element is one of the four substances (earth, air, fire, and water) from which people used to believe that everything was made.

sight [sait] n. 시야
If it is out of sight, you cannot see it.

peek [pi:k] v. (재빨리) 훔쳐보다
If you peek at something or someone, you have a quick look at them, often secretly.

rip [rip] v. 떼어 내다
If you rip something away, you remove it quickly and forcefully.

reveal [riví:l] v. 드러내 보이다
To reveal something means to make people aware of it.

leaky [lí:ki] a. 물이 새는
Something that is leaky has holes, cracks, or other faults which allow liquids and gases to pass through.

groan [groun] v. (고통·짜증으로) 신음 소리를 내다
If you groan something, you say it in a low, unhappy voice.

rush [rʌʃ] v. 서두르다; n. 세찬 움직임
If people rush to do something, they do it as soon as they can, because they are very eager to do it.

spray [sprei] v. 분사하다, 분무하다
If you spray a liquid somewhere or if it sprays somewhere, drops of the liquid cover a place or shower someone.

billow [bílou] v. (연기·구름 등이) 피어오르다
When smoke or cloud billows, it moves slowly upward or across the sky.

whisper [hwíspər] v. 속삭이다
When you whisper, you say something very quietly, using your breath rather than your throat, so that only one person can hear you.

pressure [préʃər] n. 압력
The pressure in a place or container is the force produced by the quantity of gas or liquid in that place or container.

crouch [krauʧ] v. 쭈그리고 앉다
If you are crouching, your legs are bent under you so that you are close to the ground and leaning forward slightly.

basement [béismənt] n. 지하실
A basement of a building is a room or floor that is built partly or entirely below ground level.

culvert [kʌ́lvərt] n. 지하 배수로
A culvert is a tunnel that carries water under a road.

end up idiom 결국 ~하게 되다
If someone or something ends up somewhere, they eventually arrive there, usually by accident.

recall [rikɔ́:l] v. 상기하다
If you recall something, you bring it back into your mind and remember it.

dip [dip] v. 살짝 담그다
If you dip something in a liquid, you put it into the liquid for a short time, so that only part of it is covered, and take it out again.

puddle [pʌdl] n. 웅덩이
A puddle is a small pool of liquid, especially water, that has collected on the ground.

rusty [rʌ́sti] a. 녹슨
A rusty metal object such as a car or a machine is covered with rust, which is a brown substance that forms on iron or steel when it comes into contact with water.

hint [hint] n. 극소량, 조금
A hint of something is a very small amount of it.

knock [nak] v. (움직이도록) 치다
If you knock something, you touch or hit it roughly, especially so that it falls or moves.

jam [dʒæm] v. 밀어 넣다
When something is jammed, it is roughly shoved into a place.

clog [klag] v. 막다
When something clogs a hole or place, it blocks it so that nothing can pass through.

explosion [iksplóuʒən] n. 폭발
An explosion is a sudden, violent burst of energy, for example one caused by a bomb.

vibration [vaibréiʃən] n. 진동
A vibration is a continuous shaking movement or feeling.

burst [bə:rst] v. 불쑥 움직이다
To burst into or out of a place means to enter or leave it suddenly with a lot of energy or force.

face to face idiom ~에 직면한, 대면한
If you come face to face with someone, you meet them and can talk to them or look at them directly.

exact [igzǽkt] a. 정확한
If something is exact, it means it's just right, with no mistakes.

gaze [geiz] v. 응시하다, 바라보다
To gaze at something or someone means to look steadily and intently, especially in admiration, surprise, or thought.

in the distance idiom 저 멀리, 먼 곳에 (= into the distance)
If you can see something in the distance, you can see it, far away from you.

simmer [símər] v. (속이) 부글부글 끓다
If you are simmering with anger, or if anger is simmering in you, you feel very angry but do not show your feelings.

9 & 10

1. What did Ember make to get a better view of the canals?

    A. A ladder

    B. A hot-air balloon

    C. A smoke cap

    D. A glass bubble

2. What did Ember recall when she saw Garden Central Station?

    A. She was not allowed to see a Vivisteria tree.

    B. She hung the sign about the blooming Vivisteria.

    C. Her dad used to work there as a guard.

    D. She used to live near there.

3. **How did Ember fix the leaky pipe in the shop?**

   A. She used sand to cover it up.

   B. She used different tools.

   C. She melted the pipes with her hands.

   D. She made glass to fix it.

4. **What problem did Ember have in the movie theater?**

   A. She could not find a seat.

   B. Her flames were too bright.

   C. There was no audience at the theater.

   D. The lights on the ceilings were too bright.

5. **What happened to Ember when she walked home under the elevated Wetro?**

   A. She was splashed with water.

   B. She protected herself with an umbrella.

   C. She longed to touch the water.

   D. She fell on the floor.

Check Your Reading Speed

1분에 몇 단어를 읽는지 리딩 속도를 측정해 보세요.

$$\frac{1,390 \text{ words}}{\text{reading time ( ) sec}} \times 60 = (\quad) \text{ WPM}$$

Build Your Vocabulary

rooftop [rúftàp] n. 지붕, 옥상

A rooftop is the outside part of the roof of a building.

slide [slaid] v. (slid-slid) 슬며시 움직이다

When you slide something somewhere, it moves there smoothly over or against something.

chimney [ʧímni] n. 굴뚝

A chimney is a pipe through which smoke goes up into the air, usually through the roof of a building.

top [tap] v. (다른 것의) 위에 놓다

If something is topped with something, it has that thing as its highest part.

melt [melt] v. 녹이다

When a solid substance melts or when you melt it, it changes to a liquid, usually because it has been heated.

topple [tapl] v. 넘어지다

If someone or something topples somewhere or if you topple them, they become unsteady or unstable and fall over.

yelp [jelp] v. 비명을 지르다

If a person or dog yelps, they give a sudden short cry, often because of fear or pain.

dart [da:rt] v. 쏜살같이 움직이다

If a person or animal darts somewhere, they move there suddenly and quickly.

upside-down [ʌpsàid-dáun] a. (아래위가) 거꾸로 된

If something is upside-down, it has been turned around so that the part that is usually lowest is above the part that is usually highest.

inflate [infléit] v. 부풀다
If something such as a balloon or tire inflates, it becomes bigger as it is filled with air or a gas.

makeshift [méikʃift] a. 임시의
Makeshift things are temporary and usually of poor quality, but they are used because there is nothing better available.

balloon [bəlúːn] n. 열기구 풍선
A balloon is a large bag made of strong material that is filled with hot air or gas to make it rise in the air, usually carrying a basket for passengers.

astonishment [əstániʃmənt] n. 깜짝 놀람
Astonishment is a feeling of great surprise.

exclaim [ikskléim] v. 외치다
If you exclaim, you cry out suddenly in surprise, strong emotion, or pain.

stare [stɛər] v. 빤히 쳐다보다
If you stare at someone or something, you look at them for a long time.

blaze [bleiz] n. 불꽃; v. 활활 타다
A blaze is a large fire which is difficult to control and which destroys a lot of things.

reluctantly [rilʌ́ktəntli] ad. 마지못해
If you do something reluctantly, you do it even though you do not really want to.

lean [liːn] v. (몸을) 숙이다
When you lean in a particular direction, you bend your body in that direction.

float [flout] v. (물 위나 공중에서) 떠다니다, 흘러가다
Something that floats in or through the air hangs in it or moves slowly and gently through it.

recognize [rékəgnàiz] v. 알아보다
If you recognize someone or something, you know who that person is or what that thing is.

spot [spat] n. (특정한) 장소; v. 발견하다
You can refer to a particular place as a spot.

steer [stiər] v. 조종하다
When you steer a car, boat, or plane, you control it so that it goes in the direction that you want.

darken [dá:rkən] v. 어두워지다
If something darkens or if a person or thing darkens it, it becomes darker.

illuminate [ilú:mənèit] v. 비추다
To illuminate something means to shine light on it and to make it brighter and more visible.

earth [ə:rθ] n. 흙
Earth is the substance in which plants grow that covers most of the land.

freeze [fri:z] v. (froze-frozen) (두려움 등으로 몸이) 얼어붙다
If someone who is moving freezes, they suddenly stop and become completely still and quiet.

weird [wiərd] a. 이상한
If you describe something or someone as weird, you mean that they are strange.

pruning [prú:niŋ] n. 가지치기
Pruning is the activity of cutting off some of the branches from a tree or bush so that it will grow better and stronger.

awkward [ɔ́:kwərd] a. 어색한
An awkward movement or position is uncomfortable or clumsy.

silence [sáiləns] n. 침묵
If there is silence, nobody is speaking.

inquire [inkwáiər] v. 묻다
If you inquire about something, you ask for information about it.

retire [ritáiər] v. 은퇴하다
When people retire, they leave their job and usually stop working completely.

take over idiom ~을 이어받다
If you take over a company, you get control of it.

pass [pæs] v. 사망하다
If someone passed, they died.

point [pɔint] n. 의미, 목적; v. 가리키다
If you ask what the point of something is, or say that there is no point in it, you are indicating that a particular action has no purpose or would not be useful.

embrace [imbréis] v. 받아들이다
If you embrace a change, political system, or idea, you accept it and start supporting it or believing in it.

accurately [ǽkjurətli] ad. 정확하게
If you try do something accurately, you try do it without making any mistakes.

repeat [ripíːt] v. 한 번 더 말하다
If you repeat something, you say or write it again.

slump [slʌmp] v. 구부정해지다
If your shoulders or head slump or are slumped, they bend forward because you are unhappy, tired, or unconscious.

fib [fib] v. 거짓말을 하다
If someone is fibbing, they are telling lies.

childhood [ʧáildhùd] n. 어린 시절
A person's childhood is the period of their life when they are a child.

thrive [θráiv] v. 잘 자라다
If someone or something thrives, they do well and are successful, healthy, or strong.

environment [inváiərənmənt] n. (자연) 환경
The environment is the natural world of land, sea, air, plants, and animals.

include [inklúːd] v. 포함하다
If one thing includes another thing, it has the other thing as one of its parts.

advertise [ǽdvərtàiz] v. 광고하다
If you advertise something such as a product, an event, or a job, you tell people about it online, in newspapers, on television, or on posters in order to encourage them to buy the product, go to the event, or apply for the job.

bloom [bluːm] v. 꽃이 피다
If a plant blooms, its flowers open.

grab [græb] v. 움켜잡다
If you grab something, you take it or pick it up suddenly and roughly.

entrance [éntrəns] n. 입구
An entrance is a place where you can enter a building or a place.

guard [gɑ:rd] n. 경비 요원
A guard is someone such as a soldier, police officer, or prison officer who is guarding a particular place or person.

murmur [mə́:rmə] v. 중얼거리다
If you murmur something, you say it very quietly so that not many people can hear what you are saying.

furious [fjúəriəs] a. 몹시 화가 난
Someone who is furious is extremely angry.

holler [hálər] v. 소리지르다, 고함치다
If you holler, you shout loudly.

how dare you idiom 어떻게 감히 네가!
You say 'how dare you' when you are very shocked and angry about something that someone has done.

shame on you idiom 부끄러운 줄 알아!
You can use shame in expressions such as 'shame on you' to indicate that someone ought to feel shame for something they have said or done.

embarrassed [imbǽrəst] a. 당황스러운
A person who is embarrassed feels shy, ashamed, or guilty about something.

flood [flʌd] v. 물에 잠기다
If something such as a river or a burst pipe floods an area that is usually dry or if the area floods, it becomes covered with water.

scared [skɛərd] a. 무서워하는, 겁먹은
If you are scared of someone or something, you are frightened of them.

shake off idiom ~을 떨쳐내다
If you shake off something that you do not want such as an illness or a bad habit, you manage to recover from it or get rid of it.

uncomfortable [ʌnkʌ́mfərtəbəl] a. 불쾌한
You can describe a situation or fact as uncomfortable when it is difficult to deal with and causes problems and worries.

draw [drɔ:] v. 끌어당기다, 모으다
If someone or something draws you, it attracts you very strongly.

stadium [stéidiəm] n. 경기장
A stadium is a large sports ground with rows of seats all round it.

droop [dru:p] v. 아래로 처지다
If something droops, it hangs or leans downward with no strength or firmness.

lose one's temper idiom 화를 내다
If you lose your temper, you become so angry that you shout at someone or show in some other way that you are no longer in control of yourself.

ridiculous [ridíkjuləs] a. 말도 안 되는
If you say that something or someone is ridiculous, you mean that they are very foolish.

culvert [kálvərt] n. 지하 배수로
A culvert is a tunnel that carries water under a road.

land [lænd] v. 착륙하다, 내려앉다
If a plane, bird, or insect lands, it moves safely down onto the ground.

ajar [ədʒá:r] a. 약간 열려 있는
If a door is ajar, it is slightly open.

dip [dip] v. 살짝 담그다
If you dip something in a liquid, you put it into the liquid for a short time, so that only part of it is covered, and take it out again.

nearby [nìərbái] a. 바로 가까이의
If something is nearby, it is only a short distance away.

gag [gæg] v. 구역질이 나다
If you gag, you cannot swallow and nearly vomit.

confirm [kənfə́:rm] v. 확인해 주다
If you confirm something that has been stated or suggested, you say that it is true because you know about it.

source [sɔ:rs] n. 원천, 근원
A source is where something comes from.

investigate [invéstəgèit] v. 조사하다
If someone, especially an official, investigates an event, situation, or claim, they try to find out what happened or what is the truth.

spillover [spílòuvər] n. 넘친 것
A spillover is something that is too large or too much for the place where it starts, and spreads to other places.

wake [weik] n. (배가) 지나간 흔적
The wake of a boat or other object moving in water is the track of waves that it makes
behind it as it moves through the water.

trigger [trígə:r] v. 촉발시키다
If something triggers an event or situation, it causes it to begin to happen or exist.

panic [pǽnik] v. (panicked-panicked) 어쩔 줄 모르다
If you panic or if someone panics you, you suddenly feel anxious or afraid, and act
quickly and without thinking carefully.

safety [séifti] n. 안전한 곳
If you reach safety, you reach a place where you are safe from danger.

cling [kliŋ] v. 매달리다
If you cling to something, you hold on it tightly.

desperately [déspərətli] ad. 필사적으로
If you do something desperately, you do it in a way that shows you must do something
to change it.

thrust [θrʌst] v. (thrust-thrust) (거칠게) 밀다
If you thrust something somewhere, you push or move them there quickly with a lot
of force.

grasp [græsp] v. 꽉 잡다
If you grasp something, you take it in your hand and hold it very firmly.

tug [tʌg] v. 잡아당기다
If you tug something, you pull it suddenly and strongly.

steam [sti:m] v. 증기를 내뿜다
If something steams, it gives off the gas that water produces when it is boiled.

pile [pail] n. 더미; v. 쌓다, 포개다
A pile of things is a mass of them that is high in the middle and has sloping sides.

splatter [splǽtər] v. (물·페인트 등을) 튀기다
If a liquid splatters or you splatter it, it falls onto a surface, often in many small drops.

struggle [strʌgl] v. 노력하다, 애쓰다
If you struggle to do something, you try hard to do it, even though other people or
things may be making it difficult for you to succeed.

grit [grit] v. 이를 악물다
If you grit your teeth, you press your upper and lower teeth tightly together, usually because you are angry about something.

undulate [Ándʒulèit] v. 파도 모양을 이루다
Something that undulates has gentle curves or slopes, or moves gently and slowly up and down or from side to side in an attractive manner.

pressure [préʃər] n. 압력
The pressure in a place or container is the force produced by the quantity of gas or liquid in that place or container.

heave [hi:v] v. 들어서 던지다
If you heave something heavy or difficult to move somewhere, you push, pull, or lift it using a lot of effort.

stack [stæk] v. 쌓다
If you stack up a number of things, you arrange them so that they are placed on top of one another.

in place idiom 제자리에
If something is in place, it is in the correct position.

catch one's breath idiom 한숨 돌리다
When you catch your breath while you are doing something energetic, you stop for a short time so that you can start breathing normally again.

crew [kru:] n. (함께 일을 하는) 조, 반
A crew is a group of people who work together, especially in manual labor or in a specific project.

catch [kæʧ] v. 알아듣다
If you catch something that someone has said, you manage to hear it.

distracted [distrǽktid] a. (정신이) 산만해진
When someone is distracted, it means they are unable to concentrate because their thoughts are not focused.

clump [klʌmp] n. (흙 따위의) 덩어리
A clump of something such as earth or mud is a small mass of it.

poke around idiom (무엇을 찾으려고) 뒤지다, 캐다
If you poke around, you search for something by moving things around, usually not in a very careful or organized way.

cheek [ʧiːk] n. 뺨, 볼
Your cheeks are the sides of your face below your eyes.

yank [jæŋk] v. 홱 잡아당기다
If you yank someone or something somewhere, you pull them there suddenly and with a lot of force.

pluck [plʌk] v. (잡아당겨) 빼내다
If you pluck something from somewhere, you take it between your fingers and pull it sharply from where it is.

lock [lak] v. 고정시키다
If two people's eyes lock, they look directly into each other's eyes.

blurt [bləːrt] v. 불쑥 말하다
If someone blurts something, they say it suddenly, after trying hard to keep quiet or to keep it secret.

lower [lóuər] v. (눈을) 내리깔다
If someone lowers their head or eyes, they look downward, for example because they are sad or embarrassed.

hang out idiom 많은 시간을 보내다
If you hang out in a place or with a person or a group of people, you spend a lot of time in there or with them.

insist [insíst] v. 우기다, 고집하다
To insist means to demand that something must be done or that you must have a particular thing.

grin [grin] v. 활짝 웃다
When you grin, you smile broadly.

Check Your Reading Speed
1분에 몇 단어를 읽는지 리딩 속도를 측정해 보세요.

$$\frac{972 \text{ words}}{\text{reading time ( ) sec}} \times 60 = (\quad) \text{ WPM}$$

Build Your Vocabulary

bucket [bʌ́kit] n. 양동이, 들통
A bucket is a round metal or plastic container with a handle attached to its sides.

drip [drip] v. 떨어지다
When liquid drips somewhere, or you drip it somewhere, it falls in individual small drops.

trickle [trikl] n. 물방울
A trickle of water is a small amount of liquid, flowing slowly.

snuff [snʌf] v. (불을) 끄다
If you snuff out a small flame, you stop it burning, usually by using your fingers or by covering it with something for a few seconds.

fiery [fáiəri] a. 불의, 화염의
If you describe something as fiery, you mean that it is burning strongly or contains fire.

ceiling [síːliŋ] n. 천장
A ceiling is the horizontal surface that forms the top part or roof inside a room.

leak [liːk] n. (액체·기체가) 새는 곳
A leak is a crack, hole, or other gap that a substance such as a liquid or gas can pass through.

grumble [grʌmbl] v. 투덜거리다
If someone grumbles, they complain about something in a bad-tempered way.

glance [glæns] v. 흘낏 보다
If you glance at something or someone, you look at them very quickly and then look away again immediately.

hop [hap] v. 급히 움직이다
If you hop somewhere, you move there quickly or suddenly.

leaky [líːki] a. 물이 새는
Something that is leaky has holes, cracks, or other faults which allow liquids and gases to pass through.

delivery [dilívəri] n. 배달
Delivery is the act of taking goods or letters to the person or the place they have been sent to.

sniff [snif] v. 냄새를 맡다
If you sniff something, you breathe air in through the nose in order to discover or enjoy the smell of it.

light up idiom 환해지다
If your face or your eyes light up, you suddenly look very surprised or happy.

exclaim [ikskléim] v. 외치다
If you exclaim, you cry out suddenly in surprise, strong emotion, or pain.

glee [gliː] n. 큰 기쁨
Glee is a feeling of happiness or excitement.

startle [staːrtl] v. 깜짝 놀라게 하다
If something sudden and unexpected startles you, it surprises and frightens you slightly.

announce [ənáuns] v. 큰 소리로 알리다
To announce means to say something in a loud and often serious way.

pop [pap] v. 불쑥 내놓다
If you pop something somewhere, you put it there quickly.

tiny [táini] a. 아주 작은
Tiny describes something that is very small in size or extent.

armpit [áːrmpit] n. 겨드랑이
Your armpits are the areas of your body under your arms where your arms join your shoulders.

marquee [maːrkíː] n. 대형 천막
A marquee is a large sign over a building that indicates the information about what is happening inside the builing.

tide [taid] n. 조수, 조류
The tide is the regular change in the level of the sea on the shore.

prejudice [prédʒudis] n. 편견
Prejudice is an unreasonable dislike of a particular group of people or things, or a preference for one group of people or things over another.

pull oneself together idiom 침착을 되찾다
If you are upset or depressed and someone tells you to pull yourself together, they are telling you to control your feelings and behave calmly again.

head [hed] v. (특정 방향으로) 가다
If you are heading for a particular place, you are going toward that place.

dim [dim] v. 희미해지다
If a light dims, it becomes less bright.

flame [fleim] n. 불꽃
A flame is the hot, bright, and burning gas produced by something on fire.

audience [ɔ́:diəns] n. 관중, 관객
The audience at a play, concert, film, or public meeting is the group of people watching or listening to it.

scowl [skaul] v. 얼굴을 찌푸리다
When someone scowls, an angry or hostile expression appears on their face.

slink [sliŋk] v. (slunk-slunk) 슬그머니 움직이다
If you slink somewhere, you move there quietly because you do not want to be seen.

wander [wándər] v. 거닐다
If you wander in a place, you walk around there in a casual way, often without intending to go in any particular direction.

booth [bu:θ] n. (칸막이를 한) 작은 공간
A booth is a small area separated from a larger public area by screens or thin walls.

goofy [gú:fi] a. 바보 같은
If you describe someone or something as goofy, you think they are rather silly or ridiculous.

glow [glou] n. 불빛
A glow is a dull, steady light, for example the light produced by a fire when there are no flames.

visible [vízəbl] a. (눈에) 보이는, 알아볼 수 있는
If something is visible, it can be seen.

eyeball [áibɔl] n. 안구, 눈알
Your eyeballs are your whole eyes, rather than just the part which can be seen between your eyelids.

board [bɔ:rd] v. 탑승하다
When you board a train, ship, or aircraft, you get on it in order to travel somewhere.

observation [àbzərvéiʃən] n. 관측, 관찰
Observation is the action or process of carefully watching someone or something.

crowd [kraud] v. 몰려들다
If people crowd into a place or are crowded into a place, large numbers of them enter it so that it becomes very full.

squeeze [skwi:z] v. 비집고 들어가다
If you squeeze a person or thing somewhere or if they squeeze there, they manage to get through or into a small space.

shrink [ʃriŋk] v. (shrank-shrunk) 움츠러들다
If you shrink away from someone or something, you move away from them because you are frightened, shocked, or disgusted by them.

put someone at ease idiom ~을 안심시키다
If you put someone at their ease, you make them feel relaxed and confident, not nervous or embarrassed.

transform [trænsfɔ́:rm] v. 변형시키다
To transform something into something else means to change or convert it into that thing.

silly [síli] a. 우스꽝스러운
If you say that someone or something is silly, you mean that they are foolish, childish, or ridiculous.

cheer [ʧiər] v. 환호하다
When people cheer, they shout loudly to show their approval or to encourage someone who is doing something such as taking part in a game.

bow [bau] n. (고개 숙여 하는) 인사, 절
A bow is the act of bending your head or the upper part of your body forward in order to say hello or goodbye to someone or to show respect.

adore [ədɔ́ːr] v. 흠모하다
If you adore someone, you feel great love and admiration for them.

counter [káuntər] n. 계산대
In a place such as a shop or café, a counter is a long narrow table or flat surface at which customers are served.

doodle [dúːdl] v. 낙서를 끄적거리다
To doodle means to draw little pictures or patterns on something without thinking about it.

sneak [sniːk] v. (snuck-snuck) 몰래 하다; 살금살금 가다
If you sneak a look at someone or something, you secretly have a quick look at them.

strip [strip] n. 길쭉한 조각
A strip of something such as paper, cloth, or food is a long, narrow piece of it.

tuck [tʌk] v. 끼워 넣다
If you tuck something somewhere, you push it into a small and safe place.

sparkler [spáːrklər] n. (손에 들고 터뜨리는) 폭죽
A sparkler is a small firework that you can hold as it burns.

churn [tʃəːrn] v. 마구 휘돌다
If water, mud, or dust churns, it moves about violently.

take a breath idiom 심호흡을 하다
If you say that you took a breath before doing something dangerous or frightening, you mean that you tried to make yourself feel strong and confident.

compose [kəmpóuz] v. (감정·표정 등을) 가다듬다
If you compose yourself, you succeed in becoming calm after you have been angry, excited, or upset.

steal [stiːl] v. (stole-stolen) 몰래 하다
If you steal a glance at someone or something, you look at them quickly so that nobody sees you looking.

sigh [sai] v. 한숨을 쉬다
When you sigh, you let out a deep breath, as a way of expressing feelings such as disappointment, tiredness, or pleasure.

relief [rilíːf] n. 안도, 안심
Relief is the feeling of happiness that you have when something unpleasant stops or does not happen.

aloud [əláud] ad. 큰 소리로
When you say something, read, or laugh aloud, you speak or laugh so that other people can hear you.

determined [ditə́:rmind] a. 단단히 결심한
If you are determined to do something, you have made a firm decision to do it and will not let anything stop you.

hang out idiom 많은 시간을 보내다
If you hang out in a place or with a person or a group of people, you spend a lot of time in there or with them.

outdoor [áutdɔ̀:r] a. 야외의
Outdoor activities or things happen or are used outside and not in a building.

breeze [bri:z] v. 경쾌하게 움직이다
To breeze means to move somewhere quickly in a confident way and without worrying.

mug [mʌg] n. (큰) 잔, 머그잔
A mug is a large deep cup with straight sides and a handle, used for hot drinks.

down [daun] v. 급히 다 먹다
If you say that someone downs food or a drink, you mean that they eat or drink it.

gulp [gʌlp] n. 꿀꺽 한 입
A gulp of air, food, or drink, is a large amount of it that you swallow at once.

immediately [imí:diətli] ad. 즉시
If something happens immediately, it happens without any delay.

bounce [bauns] v. (아래위로) 흔들다
If you bounce something, it swings or moves up and down.

sloshy [sláʃi] a. 출렁거리는
If something is sloshy, it moves around in an uncontrolled way.

stomach [stʌ́mək] n. 배, 복부
You can refer to the front part of your body below your waist as your stomach.

stretch [streʧ] v. (팔·다리를) 뻗다
If you stretch your arms or legs out, you move them away from your body to reach something.

stream [stri:m] n. (액체·기체의) 줄기
A stream of smoke, air, or liquid is a narrow moving mass of it.

ELEMENTAL

flickering [flíkəriŋ] a. 깜박거리는
If something such as a flame or light is flickering, it moves or shines irregularly or unsteadily.

freeze [fri:z] v. (froze-frozen) (두려움 등으로 몸이) 얼어붙다
If someone who is moving freezes, they suddenly stop and become completely still and quiet.

relieved [rilí:vd] a. 안도하는
If you are relieved, you feel happy because something unpleasant has not happend or you are not worried about something any more.

fountain [fáuntən] n. 분수
A fountain is an ornamental feature in a pool or lake which consists of a long narrow stream of water that is forced up into the air by a pump.

emerge [imə́:rdʒ] v. 나타나다
To emerge means to come out from somewhere and become possible to see.

spout [spaut] v. 내뿜다
If something spouts liquid or fire, or if liquid or fire spout out of something, it comes out very quickly with a lot of force.

statue [stǽʧu:] n. 조각상
A statue is a large sculpture of a person or an animal, made of stone or metal.

stroll [stroul] v. 거닐다
If you stroll somewhere, you walk there in a slow, relaxed way.

shore [ʃɔ:r] n. 해안가
The shore is the land along the edge of a sea, lake, or wide river.

race [reis] v. 급히 가다
If you race somewhere, you go there as quickly as possible.

out loud idiom 소리 내어
If you say something out loud, you say it so that other people can hear you.

awesome [ɔ́:səm] a. 굉장한
An awesome person or thing is very impressive and often frightening.

leap [li:p] v. 뛰어오르다
If you leap somewhere, you move there suddenly and quickly.

cluster [klʌ́stər] n. (함께 나타나는) 무리
A cluster of people or things is a small group of them close together.

surface [sə́:rfis] n. 표면
Surface is the flat top part or the outside of something.

skid [skid] v. 미끄러지다
If a person skids, it slides, usually sideways, especially on slippery ground.

mist [mist] n. 엷은 안개
Mist consists of a large number of tiny drops of water in the air, which make it difficult to see very far.

ray [rei] n. 광선
Rays of light are narrow beams of light.

reflect [riflékt] v. 반사하다
When light, heat, or other rays reflect off a surface or when a surface reflects them, they are sent back from the surface and do not pass through it.

aglow [əglóu] a. 환히 빛나는
If something is aglow, it is shining and bright with a soft, warm light.

definitely [défənitli] ad. 분명히
You use definitely to emphasize that something is the case, or to emphasize the strength of your intention or opinion.

grow on idiom ~이 점점 좋아지다
If someone or something grows on you, you start to like them more and more.

elevated [éləvèitid] a. (주변이나 지면보다) 높은
If land or buildings are elevated, they are raised up higher than the surrounding area.

whiz [hwiz] v. 윙 하며 움직이다
If something whizzes somewhere, it moves there very fast.

long [lɔːŋ] v. 간절히 바라다
If you long to do something, you want it very much.

hesitate [hézətèit] v. 망설이다, 주저하다
If you hesitate, you do not speak or act for a short time, usually because you are uncertain, embarrassed, or worried about what you are going to say or do.

vanish [vǽniʃ] v. 사라지다

If someone or something vanishes, they disappear suddenly or in a way that cannot be explained.

disappear [dìsəpíər] v. 사라지다

When someone or something disappears, you can no longer see them.

uptown [ʌptaún] ad. 도심을 벗어나

If something is uptown, it is located in a town or city that are away from the center, where people live.

11 & 12

1. Why did Wade use the water from the vases?

    A. To water the flowers

    B. To make himself taller

    C. To put out the Blue Flame

    D. To drink because he was thirsty

2. How did Bernie test if Wade really is a food inspector?

    A. He asked him to take off the badge.

    B. He asked him to clean the kitchen.

    C. He made him taste kol nuts.

    D. He quizzed him on food safety rules.

3. What did Ember create out of sand and fire?

A. A glass sphere

B. A sandcastle

C. firework

D. A wooden boat

4. What happened when a boat passed through the canal?

A. The glass wall broke.

B. The glass wall held the water back.

C. Ember and Wade got soaked.

D. The boat hit the glass wall.

5. What was Bernie doing when Ember found him downstairs?

A. Making kol nuts

B. Talking with Cinder

C. Taking a rest

D. Repairing a wall

Check Your Reading Speed

1분에 몇 단어를 읽는지 리딩 속도를 측정해 보세요.

$$\frac{1{,}397 \text{ words}}{\text{reading time ( ) sec}} \times 60 = (\quad) \text{ WPM}$$

Build Your Vocabulary

shallow [ʃǽlou] a. 얕은
A shallow container, hole, or area of water measures only a short distance from the top to the bottom.

canal [kənǽl] n. 운하
A canal is a long, narrow stretch of water that has been made for boats to travel along or to bring water to a particular area.

shelf [ʃelf] n. 선반
A shelf is a flat piece of wood, plastic, or glass that is attached to the wall or is part of a piece of furniture, used for putting things on.

rumble [rʌmbl] v. 우르릉거리는 소리를 내다
If someone or something rumbles, it makes a low, continuous noise.

chunk [ʧʌŋk] n. 덩어리
A chunk is a big piece of something.

crash [kræʃ] v. 부딪치다, 박살나다
If something crashes somewhere, it moves and hits something else violently, making a loud noise.

gush [gʌʃ] v. 솟구치다
When liquid gushes out of something, or when something gushes a liquid, the liquid flows out very quickly and in large quantities.

hop [hap] v. 급히 움직이다
If you hop somewhere, you move there quickly or suddenly.

desperate [déspərət] a. 간절히 원하는
If you are desperate to do something, you want or need it very much indeed.

cough [kɔːf] v. 기침하다
When you cough, you force air out of your throat with a sudden, harsh noise.

leaky [líːki] a. 물이 새는
Something that is leaky has holes, cracks, or other faults which allow liquids and gases to pass through.

delivery [dilívəri] n. 배달
Delivery is the act of taking goods or letters to the person or the place they have been sent to.

giddy [gídi] a. 들뜬
If you feel giddy with delight or excitement, you feel so happy or excited that you find it hard to think or act normally.

gasp [gæsp] v. 헉 하고 숨을 쉬다
When you gasp, you take a short quick breath through your mouth, especially when you are surprised or shocked.

dart [daːrt] v. 쏜살같이 움직이다
If a person or animal darts somewhere, they move there suddenly and quickly.

basement [béismənt] n. 지하실
A basement of a building is a room or floor that is built partly or entirely below ground level.

whisper [hwíspər] v. 속삭이다
When you whisper, you say something very quietly, using your breath rather than your throat, so that only one person can hear you.

pour [pɔːr] v. 붓다, 쏟다
If you pour a liquid or other substance, you make it flow steadily out of a container by holding the container at an angle.

fill out idiom 더 커지다
If someone or something fills out, they become larger, rounder or fatter.

obviously [ábviəsli] ad. 명백히
You use obviously to indicate that something is easily noticed, seen, or recognized.

toss [tɔːs] v. 던지다
If you toss something, you throw it into the air with a quick, forceful motion.

detail [díːteil] n. 세부 사항
You can refer to the small features of something which are often not noticed as detail.

crew [kruː] n. (함께 일을 하는) 조, 반
A crew is a group of people who work together, especially in manual labor or in a specific project.

boss [bɔːs] n. 상사
A boss is someone who is in charge and can give orders to others.

remind [rimáind] v. 상기시키다
If someone reminds you of a fact or event that you already know about, they say something which makes you think about it.

knock [nak] v. (움직이도록) 치다
If you knock something, you touch or hit it roughly, especially so that it falls or moves.

recover [rikʌ́vər] v. 회복하다
To recover is to return to a normal state of health, mind, or strength after a physical or mental illness, injury, or shock.

picture [píkʧər] v. (마음속에) 그리다
If you picture something in your mind, you think of it and have such a clear idea of it that you seem to be able to see it.

construction [kənstrʌ́kʃən] n. 건설, 공사
Construction is the building of things such as houses, factories, roads, and bridges.

statue [stǽʧuː] n. 조각상
A statue is a large sculpture of a person or an animal, made of stone or metal.

coat [kout] v. (막 같은 것을) 덮다
If you coat something with a substance or in a substance, you cover it with a thin layer of the substance.

eventually [ivénʧuəli] ad. 결국
Eventually means at the end of a situation or process or as the final result of it.

harden [haːrdn] v. 굳다
When something hardens or when you harden it, it becomes stiff or firm.

chuckle [ʧʌkl] v. 싱긋 웃다
When you chuckle, you laugh quietly.

deadline [dédlain] n. 기한
A deadline is a time or date before which a particular task must be finished or a particular thing must be done.

exasperated [igzǽspərèitid] a. 몹시 화가 난
If you describe a person as exasperated, you mean that they are frustrated or angry because of something that is happening or something that another person is doing.

burst [bə:rst] v. (burst-burst) 갑자기 ~하다; 터지다, 파열하다
When a door or lid bursts open, it opens very suddenly and violently because someone pushes it or there is great pressure behind it.

confused [kənfjú:zd] a. 혼란스러워하는
If you are confused, you do not know what to think or what to do.

swing [swiŋ] v. (swung-swung) 휘두르다
If you swing at a person or thing, you try to hit them with your arm or with something that you are holding.

yell [jel] v. 소리치다
If you yell, you shout loudly, usually because you are excited, angry, or in pain.

badge [bædʒ] n. 신분증, 명찰
A badge is a piece of metal or cloth which you wear to show that you belong to an organization or support a cause.

inspector [inspéktər] n. 조사관
An inspector is a person, usually employed by a government agency, whose job is to find out whether people are obeying official regulations.

busted [bΛstid] a. 들통난
If you say someone is busted, it means they have been caught in the act of doing something wrong and likely to be punished.

shoot [ʃu:t] v. (shot-shot) (눈길 등을) 획 던지다
If you shoot a look at someone, you look at them quickly and briefly, often in a way that expresses your feelings.

play along idiom 동의하는 척하다
If you play along with a person, with what they say, or with their plans, you appear to agree with them and do what they want, even though you are not sure whether they are right.

confirm [kənfɔ́:rm] v. 확인해 주다
If you confirm something that has been stated or suggested, you say that it is true because you know about it.

uncertainly [ʌnsə́rtənli] ad. 확신 없이, 머뭇거리며
If you do something uncertainly, you do it without confidence.

magnify [mǽgnəfài] v. 확대하다
To magnify an object means to make it appear larger than it really is, by means of a special lens or mirror.

poke around idiom (무엇을 찾으려고) 뒤지다, 캐다
If you poke around, you search for something by moving things around, usually not in a very careful or organized way.

fumble [fʌmbl] v. (말을) 더듬거리다
When you are trying to say something, if you fumble for the right words, you speak in a clumsy and unclear way.

inspect [inspékt] v. 면밀하게 살피다, 점검하다
If you inspect something, you look at every part of it carefully in order to find out about it or check that it is all right.

official [əfíʃəl] a. (직책과 관련된) 공식적인
Official means approved by the government or by someone in authority.

hiss [his] v. (강한 어조로) 낮게 말하다; 쉬익 하는 소리를 내다
If you hiss something, you say it forcefully in a whisper.

grunt [grʌnt] v. 끙 앓는 소리를 내다
If you grunt, you make a low sound, especially because you are annoyed or not interested in something.

frustration [frʌstréiʃən] n. 좌절감
Frustration is a feeling you get when you can't do or get what you want.

slam [slæm] v. 세게 놓다
If you slam something down, you put it there quickly and with great force.

nervously [nɔ́:rvəsli] ad. 초조하게
If you do something nervously, you do it while feeling worried or not relaxed.

interrogate [intérəgèit] v. 심문하다, 캐묻다
If someone interrogates someone, they question them thoroughly for a long time in order to get some information from them.

gesture [dʒéstʃər] v. 가리키다, 몸짓을 하다
If you gesture, you use movements of your hands or head in order to tell someone something or draw their attention to something.

silence [sáiləns] v. 조용히 하게 하다
To silence someone or something means to stop them speaking or making a noise.

nostril [nástrəl] n. 콧구멍
Your nostrils are the two openings at the end of your nose.

demonstrate [démənstrèit] v. (행동으로) 보여 주다
If you demonstrate a particular skill, quality, or feeling, you show by your actions that you have it.

scoop [sku:p] v. 푸다, 뜨다
If you scoop something up, you put your hands or arms under it and lift it in a quick movement.

hold one's breath idiom 숨을 죽이다
If you say that someone is holding their breath, you mean that they are waiting anxiously or excitedly for something to happen.

scalding [skɔ́:ldiŋ] a. 델 정도로 뜨거운
Scalding or scalding hot liquids are extremely hot.

bite [bait] n. 한 입
A bite of something, especially food, is the action of using someone's teeth to cut or break something, usually in order to eat it.

sizzle [sizl] v. 지글지글하는 소리를 내다
If something such as hot oil or fat sizzles, it makes hissing sounds.

let out idiom (소리를) 내다
If you let out a particular sound, you make that sound.

clamp [klæmp] v. 꽉 잡다
To clamp something in a particular place means to put it or hold it there firmly and tightly.

satisfied [sǽtisfàid] a. 만족스러운
If you are satisfied, it means you are pleased because you have what you want, or because something has happened in the way that you want.

smirk [smə:rk] n. 능글맞은 웃음
A smirk is a silly and unpleasant smile that shows that you are pleased with yourself, know something that other people do not know.

massive [mǽsiv] a. 거대한
Something that is massive is very large in size, quantity, or extent.

steam [sti:m] n. 증기
Steam is the gas that water produces when you heat it.

nod [nad] v. (고개를) 끄덕이다
If you nod, you move your head up and down to show agreement, understanding, or approval.

caution [kɔ́ːʃən] v. 주의를 주다
If someone cautions you, they warn you about problems or danger.

croak [krouk] v. 목이 쉰 듯 말하다
If someone croaks something, they say it in a low, rough voice.

straighten [streitn] v. (자세를) 바로 하다
When you straighten up, you make your body upright from a relaxed or bent position.

die down idiom 차츰 약해지다
If something dies down, it becomes very much quieter or less intense.

portion [pɔ́ːrʃən] n. 1인분
A portion is the amount of food that is given to one person at a meal.

smolder [smóuldər] v. (서서히) 타다
If something smolders, it burns slowly, producing smoke but not flames.

clear one's throat idiom 목을 가다듬다
If you clear your throat, you cough once in order to make it easier to speak or to attract people's attention.

attention [əténʃən] n. 주의, 주목
If you give someone or something your attention, you look at it, listen to it, or think about it carefully.

slide [slaid] v. (slid-slid) 슬며시 움직이다
When you slide something somewhere, it moves there smoothly over or against something.

mug [mʌg] n. (큰) 잔, 머그잔
A mug is a large deep cup with straight sides and a handle, used for hot drinks.

smack one's lips idiom 입맛을 다시다
If you smack your lips, you open and close your mouth noisily, especially before or after eating, to show that you are eager to eat or enjoyed eating.

water down idiom ~을 약화시키다
If you water down something, you make it less effective or powerful.

explode [iksplóud] v. (감정이) 폭발하다
If someone explodes, they express strong feelings suddenly and violently.

instant [ínstənt] a. 즉각적인
You use instant to describe something that happens immediately.

snap [snæp] v. 사진을 찰칵 찍다
If you snap someone or something, you take a photograph of them.

terrified [térəfàid] a. 겁에 질린
If you are terrified, you are very frightened.

declare [diklέər] v. 분명히 말하다
If you declare that something is true, you say that it is true in a firm, deliberate way.

huff [hʌf] v. (화가 나서) 씩씩거리다
If you huff, you indicate that you are annoyed or offended about something, usually by the way that you say something.

glare [glέər] v. 노려보다
When you glare at someone, you look at them with an angry expression on your face.

let loose idiom (갑자기 시끄러운 소리·말을) 내뱉다
To let loose something means to make a sound or remark suddenly.

figure out idiom 알아내다
If you figure out a solution to a problem or the reason for something, you succeed in solving it or understanding it.

lock [lak] v. 고정시키다
If two people's eyes lock, they look directly into each other's eyes.

seethe [si:ð] v. (분노 등이) 부글거리다
When you are seething, you are very angry about something but do not express your feelings about it.

pin [pin] v. (핀으로) 고정시키다
If you pin something on or to something, you attach it with a pin.

ban [bæn] v. 금지하다
To ban something means to state officially that it must not be done, shown, or used.

gently [dʒéntli] ad. 부드럽게
Gently means in a kind, mild, or careful manner.

echo [ékou] v. 그대로 따라 하다
If you echo someone's words, you repeat them or express agreement with their attitude or opinion.

agitated [ǽdʒitèitid] a. 흥분한
If someone is agitated, they are very worried or upset, and show this in their behavior, movements, or voice.

intensely [inténsli] ad. 격하게, 심하게
If something happens intensely, it happens with extreme strength or degree.

rush [rʌʃ] v. 서두르다
If people rush to do something, they do it as soon as they can, because they are very eager to do it.

comfort [kʌ́mfərt] v. 위로하다
If you comfort someone, you make them feel less worried, unhappy, or upset, for example by saying kind things to them.

soothe [suːð] v. 달래다
If you soothe someone who is angry or upset, you make them feel calmer.

Check Your Reading Speed

1분에 몇 단어를 읽는지 리딩 속도를 측정해 보세요.

$$\frac{942 \text{ words}}{\text{reading time ( ) sec}} \times 60 = (\quad) \text{ WPM}$$

Build Your Vocabulary

shovel [ʃʌ́vəl] v. 삽질하다, 삽으로 옮기다
If you shovel earth, coal, or snow, you lift and move it with a tool with a long handle.

exhausting [igzɔ́:stiŋ] a. 피로하게 하는
Something that is exhausting makes you extremely tired and without energy.

determined [ditə́:rmind] a. 결심한
If you are determined, you have made a firm decision to do it and you will not let anything stop you.

confess [kənfés] v. 고백하다, 인정하다
If you confess something, you admit something that you feel embarrassed about.

adjust [ədʒʌ́st] v. (매무새 등을) 바로잡다
If you adjust something such as your clothing or a machine, you correct or alter its position or setting.

scoff [skɔ:f] v. 비웃다
If you scoff at something, you speak about it in a way that shows you think it is ridiculous or inadequate.

tough [tʌf] a. 힘든, 어려운
A tough task or problem is difficult to do or solve.

regret [rigrét] n. 후회
Regret is a feeling of sadness or disappointment, which is caused by something that has happened or something that you have done or not done.

shut down idiom (공장·가게의) 문을 닫다
If a factory or business shuts down or if someone shuts it down, work there stops or it no longer trades as a business.

furious [fjúəriəs] a. 몹시 화가 난
Someone who is furious is extremely angry.

collapse [kəlǽps] v. 주저앉다
If you collapse onto something, you sit or lie down suddenly because you are very tired.

simmer [símər] v. (속이) 부글부글 끓다
If you are simmering with anger, or if anger is simmering in you, you feel very angry but do not show your feelings.

prismatic [prizmǽtik] a. 선명한
If something is prismatic, it is very bright and clear.

inner [ínər] a. 내부의
Inner is used to describe something that is inside or contained within something else.

murmur [mə́:rmə] v. 중얼거리다
If you murmur something, you say it very quietly so that not many people can hear what you are saying.

retire [ritáiər] v. 은퇴하다
When people retire, they leave their job and usually stop working completely.

endure [indjúər] v. 견디다
If you endure a painful or difficult situation, you experience it and do not avoid it or give up, usually because you cannot.

pause [pɔːz] v. 잠시 멈추다
If you pause while you are doing something, you stop for a short period and then continue.

repay [ripéi] v. 보답하다
If you repay a favor that someone did for you, you do something for them in return.

sacrifice [sǽkrəfais] n. 희생
If you sacrifice something that is valuable or important, you give it up, usually to obtain something else for yourself or for other people.

burden [bə́:rdn] n. 짐, 부담
If you describe a problem or a responsibility as a burden, you mean that it causes someone a lot of difficulty, worry, or hard work.

sink [siŋk] v. (sank-sunk) 주저앉다
If you sink, you move into a lower position, for example by sitting down in a chair or kneeling.

crouch [krauʧ] v. 쭈그리고 앉다
If you are crouching, your legs are bent under you so that you are close to the ground and leaning forward slightly.

mess [mes] n. 엉망인 상태
If you say that a situation is a mess, you mean that it is full of trouble or problems.

vulnerable [vʌ́lnərəbl] a. 약한
Something that is vulnerable can be easily harmed or affected by something bad.

grin [grin] v. 활짝 웃다
When you grin, you smile broadly.

admit [ædmít] v. 인정하다
If you admit something, you agree, often unwillingly, that it is true.

melt [melt] v. 녹이다
When a solid substance melts or when you melt it, it changes to a liquid, usually because it has been heated.

sphere [sfiər] n. 구(球), 구체
A sphere is an object that is completely round in shape like a ball.

reflect [riflékt] v. 나타내다, 반영하다
If something reflects an attitude or situation, it shows that the attitude or situation exists or it shows what it is like.

mesmerize [mézməràiz] v. 마음을 사로잡다
If you are mesmerized by something, you are so interested in it or so attracted to it that you cannot think about anything else.

seal [siːl] v. 밀폐하다, 틈을 막다
If you seal a container or an opening, you cover it with something in order to prevent air, liquid, or other material getting in or out.

culvert [kʌ́lvərt] n. 지하 배수로
A culvert is a tunnel that carries water under a road.

stack [stæk] n. 더미
A stack of things is a pile of them.

inhale [inhéil] v. 숨을 들이마시다
When you inhale, you breathe in.

explosion [iksplóuʒən] n. 폭발
An explosion is a sudden, violent burst of energy, for example one caused by a bomb.

blast [blæst] n. 폭발
A blast is a big explosion, especially one caused by a bomb.

admire [ædmáiər] v. 감탄하며 바라보다
If you admire someone or something, you look at them with pleasure.

radiant [réidiənt] a. 빛나는
Something that is radiant glows brightly.

catch one's breath idiom 한숨 돌리다
When you catch your breath while you are doing something energetic, you stop for a short time so that you can start breathing normally again.

satisfaction [sætisfǽkʃən] n. 만족감
Satisfaction is the pleasure that you feel when you do something or get something that you wanted or needed to do or get.

bite [bait] v. (bit-bitten) (이빨로) 물다
If you bite something, you use your teeth to cut into it, for example in order to eat it or break it.

sniffle [snifl] v. 훌쩍거리다
When someone sniffles, they make soft, quiet sounds, usually because they are crying.

tease [ti:z] v. 놀리다
To tease someone means to laugh at them or make jokes about them in order to embarrass, annoy, or upset them.

sob [sab] v. 흐느끼며 말하다
If you sob something, you say it while you are crying.

punch [pʌntʃ] v. 주먹으로 치다
If you punch someone or something, you hit them hard with your fist.

earth [ə:rθ] n. 땅, 지면
The earth is the land surface on which we live and move about.

vibrate [váibreit] v. 흔들리다
When something vibrates, it shakes repeatedly and quickly, often felt as rhythmic movement.

enormous [inɔ́:rməs] a. 거대한
Something that is enormous is extremely large in size or amount.

sheet [ʃi:t] n. (불·물 등의) 가득 퍼짐
A sheet of fire or water is a fast-moving mass of it that is difficult to see through.

stare [stɛər] v. 빤히 쳐다보다
If you stare at someone or something, you look at them for a long time.

splash [splæʃ] v. 철벅 떨어지다
If a liquid splashes, it hits someone or something and scatters in a lot of small drops.

creation [kriéiʃən] n. 창작물
You can refer to something that someone has made as a creation, especially if it shows skill, imagination, or artistic ability.

repair [ripέər] v. 수리하다
If you repair something that has been damaged or is not working properly, you fix it.

stern [stə:rn] a. 근엄한
Stern words or actions are very severe.

expression [ikspréʃən] n. 표정
Your expression is the way that your face looks at a particular moment.

salute [səlú:t] v. 경례하다
When you salute someone, you greet or show respect to them, often by raising your hand to your forehead.

spit [spit] v. (spat/spit-spat/spit) 내뱉듯이 말하다
If someone spits an insult or comment, they say it in an angry or hostile way.

prove [pru:v] v. 입증하다, 증명하다
If you prove that something is true, you show by means of argument or evidence that it is definitely true.

flicker [flíkər] v. (불·빛 등이) 깜박거리다
If a light or flame flickers, it shines unsteadily.

fade [feid] v. 서서히 사라지다
If someone's smile fades, they slowly stop smiling.

ban [bæn] v. 금지하다
To ban something means to state officially that it must not be done, shown, or used.

13 & 14

1. What did Ember do when Alan accidentally broke the pitcher?

  A. She bought a new one.

  B. She cast rainbows on it.

  C. She used fire to fix it.

  D. She called for help.

2. What did Wade say to Ember during the game?

  A. He asked her to leave.

  B. He confessed his love for her.

  C. He could not say anything.

  D. He said they were running out of time.

3. What broke the silence at the end?

A. A door slamming

B. The phone ringing

C. An alarm going off

D. The sound of weeping

4. Why was Ember worried about the job offer?

A. Her father needed her.

B. Her skills were not enough for the job.

C. She did not want to work.

D. She did not like places far away.

5. What did Bernie announce to Ember and Cinder?

A. That he forgot to make a new sign

B. That he is opening a new shop

C. That he is moving away

D. That he is retiring

Check Your Reading Speed

1분에 몇 단어를 읽는지 리딩 속도를 측정해 보세요.

$$\frac{1{,}834 \text{ words}}{\text{reading time ( ) sec}} \times 60 = (\quad) \text{ WPM}$$

Build Your Vocabulary

sniff [snif] v. 냄새를 맡다
If you sniff something, you breathe air in through the nose in order to discover or enjoy the smell of it.

declare [diklέər] v. 분명히 말하다
If you declare that something is true, you say that it is true in a firm, deliberate way.

lock [lak] v. (자물쇠로) 잠그다
When you lock something such as a door, drawer, or case, you fasten it, usually with a key, so that other people cannot open it.

sneak [sni:k] v. (snuck-snuck) 살금살금 가다
If you sneak somewhere, you go there very quietly on foot, trying to avoid being seen or heard.

suspiciously [səspíʃəsli] ad. 수상쩍다는 듯이
You can use suspiciously when you are describing something that you think is slightly strange or not as it should be.

head [hed] v. (특정 방향으로) 가다
If you are heading for a particular place, you are going toward that place.

scent [sent] n. 냄새
The scent of something is the pleasant smell that it has.

canal [kənal] n. 운하
A canal is a long, narrow stretch of water that has been made for boats to travel along or to bring water to a particular area.

stream [stri:m] v. 흘러가다
If a liquid streams somewhere, it flows or comes out in large amounts.

skyward [skáiwərd] ad. 하늘을 향해
If you look skyward, you look up toward the sky.

glance [glæns] v. 흘깃 보다
If you glance at something or someone, you look at them very quickly and then look away again immediately.

grand [grænd] a. 웅장한
If you describe a building or a piece of scenery as grand, you mean that its size or appearance is very impressive.

entrance [éntrəns] n. 입구
An entrance is a place where you can enter a building or a place.

surround [səráund] v. 둘러싸다
If a person or thing is surrounded by something, that thing is located all around them.

cascade [kæskéid] v. 폭포처럼 흐르다
If water cascades somewhere, it pours or flows downward very fast and in large quantities.

waterfall [wɔ́:tərfɔ:l] n. 폭포
A waterfall is a place where water flows over the edge of a steep, high cliff in hills or mountains, and falls into a pool below.

gulp [gʌlp] v. 침을 꿀꺽 삼키다
If you gulp, you swallow air, often making a noise in your throat as you do so, because you are nervous or excited.

mustache [mʌ́stæʃ] n. 콧수염
A mustache is the hair growing on the upper lip somone's face.

guard [ga:rd] v. 지키다, 보호하다
If you guard a place, person, or object, you stand near them in order to watch and protect them.

swear [swɛər] v. (swore-sworn) 맹세하다
If you swear to do something, you promise in a serious way that you will do it.

hesitate [hézətèit] v. 망설이다, 주저하다
If you hesitate, you do not speak or act for a short time, usually because you are uncertain, embarrassed, or worried about what you are going to say or do.

hot on one's trail idiom ~을 바짝 뒤쫓아
If you say that someone is hot on your trail, you are emphasizing that they are chasing you and are not very far behind you.

duck [dʌk] v. 휙 수그리다
If you duck, you move your head or the top half of your body quickly downward to avoid something that might hit you, or to avoid being seen.

peer [piər] v. 유심히 보다
If you peer at something, you look at it very hard, usually because it is difficult to see clearly.

ledge [ledʒ] n. (튀어나온) 턱
A ledge is a narrow, flat surface sticking out from a wall, cliff, or other surface.

gaze [geiz] v. 응시하다, 바라보다
To gaze at something or someone means to look steadily and intently, especially in admiration, surprise, or thought.

ritzy [rítsi] a. 호화로운
If you describe something as ritzy, you mean that it is fashionable or expensive.

shrug [ʃrʌg] v. (어깨를) 으쓱하다
If you shrug, you raise your shoulders and then drop them to show that you do not know or care about something.

resident [rézədnt] n. 거주자
The residents of a house or area are the people who live there.

spin [spin] v. (spun-spun) (휙) 돌다; 돌리다
If something spins or if you spin it, it turns quickly around a central point.

dodge [dadʒ] v. (몸을) 피하다, 비키다
If you dodge something, you avoid it by quickly moving aside or out of reach so that it cannot hit or reach you.

extend [iksténd] v. 뻗다
If you extend a part of your body, especially an arm or a leg, you stretch it away from yourself.

block [blak] v. 막다, 차단하다
If you block someone's way, you prevent them from going somewhere or entering a place by standing in front of them.

flame [fleim] n. 불꽃
A flame is the hot, bright, and burning gas produced by something on fire.

widen [waidn] v. (놀람 등으로) 둥그레지다
If your eyes widen, they open more.

greet [griːt] v. 인사하다, 맞이하다
To greet someone means to say hello to them or to welcome them.

elegant [éligənt] a. 우아한
If you describe a person or thing as elegant, you mean that they are pleasing and graceful in appearance or style.

lean [liːn] v. (몸을) 숙이다
When you lean in a particular direction, you bend your body in that direction.

put out idiom (불을) 끄다
If you put out a fire, you make it stop burning.

smitten [smítn] a. ~에게 반한
If you are smitten, you find someone so attractive that you are or seem to be in love with them.

mortify [mɔ́ːrtəfài] a. 몹시 당황한
If someone is mortified, they are feeling very ashamed or embarrassed.

light up idiom 환하게 만들다
If you light something up, it becomes bright, usually when you shine light on it.

smoky [smóuki] a. 연기가 나는
Smoky describes something filled with or smelling of smoke.

fake [feik] v. ~인 척하다
If you fake a feeling, emotion, or reaction, you pretend that you are experiencing it when you are not.

float [flout] v. (물 위나 공중에서) 떠다니다, 흘러가다
If something or someone is floating in a liquid, they are in the liquid, on or just below the surface, and are being supported by it.

furniture [fɔ́ːrniʧər] n. 가구
Furniture consists of large objects such as tables, chairs, or beds that are used in a room for sitting or lying on or for putting things on or in.

element [éləmənt] n. 원소
An element is one of the four substances (earth, air, fire, and water) from which people used to believe that everything was made.

floaty [flóuti] a. 뜨는, 뜰 수 있는
A floaty object is able to float on a liquid.

flammable [flǽməbl] a. 불에 잘 타는
Flammable chemicals, gases, cloth, or other things catch fire and burn easily.

foyer [fɔ́iər] n. 현관
The foyer is an entrance hall in a private house.

make it idiom 가다
If you make it to somewhere, you succeed in reaching there.

wobble [wabl] v. 흔들리다
If something or someone wobbles, they make small movements from side to side, for example because they are unsteady.

precariously [prikéəriəsli] ad. 위험하게
If something is done precariously, it is done in a manner that not secure and likely to fall.

exclaim [ikskléim] v. 외치다
If you exclaim, you cry out suddenly in surprise, strong emotion, or pain.

immediately [imí:diətli] ad. 즉시
If something happens immediately, it happens without any delay.

blubber [blʌ́bər] v. 흐느껴 울다
If someone blubbers, they cry noisily and in an unattractive way.

emerge [imɔ́:rdʒ] v. 나타나다
To emerge means to come out from somewhere and become possible to see.

inflatable [infléitəbl] a. (공기로) 부풀리게 되어 있는
An inflatable object is one that you fill with air when you want to use it.

apron [éiprən] n. 앞치마
An apron is a piece of clothing that you put on over the front of your normal clothes and tie round your waist.

cheery [ʧíəri] a. 쾌활한
If you describe a person or their behavior as cheery, you mean that they are cheerful and happy.

pop [pap] v. 불쑥 나타나다
If someone or something pops, it appears suddenly or unexpectedly.

holler [hálər] v. 소리지르다, 고함치다
If you holler, you shout loudly.

jostle [dʒasl] v. 거칠게 밀치다
If people jostle you, they bump against you or push you in a way that annoys you, usually because you are in a crowd and they are trying to get past you.

scold [skould] v. 야단치다
If you scold someone, you speak angrily to them because they have done something wrong.

flush [flʌʃ] v. (얼굴이) 붉어지다
If you flush, your face goes red because you are hot or ill, or because you are feeling a strong emotion such as embarrassment or anger.

embarrassment [imbǽrəsmənt] n. 당황스러움, 난처함
Embarrassment is a feeling of being shy, ashamed, or guilty about something.

regain [rigéin] v. 되찾다
If you regain something that you have lost, you get it back again.

sib [sib] n. (한 명의) 형제자매
A sib refers to one brother or sister you have.

follow in one's wake idiom 뒤따르다, 전철을 밟다
If you are following in someone's wake, you are following them or their example.

nonsense [nánsens] int. 당치도 않은 소리!, 말도 안 돼!
If you say that something spoken or written is 'nonsense', you mean that you consider it to be untrue or silly.

architect [árkətèkt] n. 건축가
An architect is a person who designs buildings.

dabble [dæbl] v. (취미 삼아) 조금 해 보다
If you dabble in something, you take part in it but not very seriously.

permanent [pə́ːrmənənt] a. 영구적인
Something that is permanent lasts for a long time or for all time in the future.

collection [kəlékʃən] n. 소장품
A collection of things is a group of similar things that you have deliberately acquired, usually over a period of time.

talent [tǽlənt] n. 재능
Talent is the natural ability to do something well.

aisle [ail] n. 통로, 복도
An aisle is a long narrow gap that people can walk along between rows of seats in a public building.

scoff [skɔːf] v. 비웃다
If you scoff at something, you speak about it in a way that shows you think it is ridiculous or inadequate.

modest [mádist] a. 겸손한
If you say that someone is modest, you approve of them because they do not talk much about their abilities or achievements.

incredible [inkrédəbl] a. 굉장한
If you say that something is incredible, you mean that it is very unusual or surprising, and you cannot believe it is really true, although it may be.

creative [kriéitiv] a. 창의적인
If something is creative, it involves the use of skill and the imagination to produce something new or a work of art.

cast [kæst] v. (cast-cast) (시선·미소 등을) 던지다
If you cast your eyes or cast a look in a particular direction, you look quickly in that direction.

keep one's cool idiom 침착함을 유지하다
If you keep your cool, you try to stay calm and not get upset or angry.

embarrassed [imbǽrəst] a. 당황스러운
A person who is embarrassed feels shy, ashamed, or guilty about something.

inappropriate [inəpróupriət] a. 부적절한
Something that is inappropriate is not useful or suitable for a particular situation or purpose.

comment [kɑ́ment] n. 논평, 언급
A comment is something that you say which expresses your opinion of something or which gives an explanation of it.

subject [sʌ́bdʒikt] n. 주제
The subject of something such as a conversation, letter, or book is the thing that is being discussed or written about.

tension [ténʃən] n. 긴장감
Tension is a feeling of nervousness that makes you unable to relax or emotional strain or suspense.

deathly [déθli] ad. 극도로
If you say that someone is deathly afraid, you are emphasizing that they are very afraid.

intrigued [intríːgd] a. 아주 흥미로워하는
If you are intrigued, you are very interested in something and wanting to know more about it.

traumatized [tráumətàizd] a. 정신적 충격을 받은
If someone is traumatized by an event or situation, it shocks or upsets them very much, and may cause them psychological damage.

kindergartner [kíndərgàːrtnər] n. 유치원생
A kindergartner is a child who is in kindergarten.

janitor [dʒǽnitər] n. 관리인
A janitor is a person whose job is to look after a building.

suck [sʌk] v. (액체·공기 등을) 빨아들이다
If something sucks a liquid, gas, or object in a particular direction, it draws it there with a powerful force.

panic [pǽnik] v. 어쩔 줄 모르다
If you panic or if someone panics you, you suddenly feel anxious or afraid, and act quickly and without thinking carefully.

suction [sʌ́kʃən] n. 빨아들임
Suction is the process by which liquids, gases, or other substances are drawn out of somewhere.

soak [souk] v. 빨아들이다, 흡수하다
If a soft or dry material soaks up a liquid, the liquid goes into the substance.

entirely [intáiərli] ad. 완전히
Entirely means completely and not just partly.

let out idiom (소리를) 내다
If you let out a particular sound, you make that sound.

chuckle [ʧʌkl] n. 킬킬 웃음
A chuckle is an act of laughing quietly.

stuck [stʌk] a. 움직일 수 없는, 꼼짝 못하는
If you are stuck in a place, you want to get away from it, but are unable to.

defensively [difénsivli] ad. 방어적으로
If something is done defensively, it is done in a manner that shows you want to protect yourself.

pitcher [píʧər] n. 물 주전자
A pitcher is a container for holding and pouring out liquids.

slip [slip] v. 미끄러지다
If something slips, it slides out of place or out of your hand.

shatter [ʃǽtər] v. 산산조각 나다
If something shatters or is shattered, it breaks into a lot of small pieces.

apologize [əpálədʒàiz] v. 사과하다
To apologize means to express regret for something wrong that one has done.

shard [ʃɑːrd] n. (유리 등의) 조각
Shards are pieces of broken glass, pottery, or metal.

reassure [riːəʃúər] v. 안심시키다
If you reassure someone, you say or do things to make them stop worrying about something.

gather [gǽðər] v. 모으다, 챙기다
If you gather things, you collect them together so that you can use them.

orb [ɔːrb] n. 구(球), 구체
An orb is something that is shaped like a ball, for example the sun or moon.

resemble [rizémbl] v. 비슷하다
If one thing or person resembles another, they are similar to each other.

inner [ínər] a. 내부의
Inner is used to describe something that is inside or contained within something else.

barely [béərli] ad. 거의 ~아니게
You use barely to say that something almost does not happen or exist.

twist [twist] n. (손으로) 돌리기, 비틀기
A twist is the action of turning something with your hand so that it moves around in a circular direction.

tweak [twiːk] v. 잡아당기다
If you tweak something, especially part of someone's body, you hold it between your finger and thumb and twist it or pull it.

spout [spaut] n. (주전자 등의) 주둥이
A spout is a long, hollow part of a container through which liquids can be poured out easily.

gush [gʌʃ] v. 마구 표현하다
If someone gushes, they express their admiration or pleasure in an exaggerated way.

cheer [ʧiər] v. 환호하다
When people cheer, they shout loudly to show their approval or to encourage someone who is doing something such as taking part in a game.

applaud [əplɔ́ːd] v. 박수를 치다
When a group of people applaud, they clap their hands in order to show approval, for example when they have enjoyed a play or concert.

modestly [mádistli] ad. 겸손하게
If someone says something modestly, they say it in a way that does not praise your own abilities or possessions.

echo [ékou] v. 그대로 따라 하다
If you echo someone's words, you repeat them or express agreement with their attitude or opinion.

admire [ædmáiər] v. 감탄하며 바라보다
If you admire someone or something, you look at them with pleasure.

district [dístrikt] n. 구역
A district is a particular area of a town or country.

have a point idiom 일리가 있다
If you say that someone has a point, you mean that you accept that what they have said is important and should be considered.

announce [ənáuns] v. 큰 소리로 알리다
To announce means to say something in a loud and often serious way.

face off idiom 경기를 시작하다
To face off means to start a game such as ice hockey.

flip [flip] v. 뒤집다
If something flips over, or if you flip it over or into a different position, it moves or is moved into a different position.

hourglass [aúərglæs] n. 모래시계
An hourglass is a device that was used to measure the passing of an hour.

instantly [ínstəntli] ad. 즉시
If something happens instantly, it happens at once.

celebrate [séləbrèit] v. 축하하다
If you celebrate, you do something enjoyable because of a special occasion or to mark someone's success.

bawl [bɔ́:l] v. 고함치다
If you bawl, you shout in a very loud voice, for example because you are angry or you want people to hear you.

unfair [ʌnfér] a. 부당한, 불공평한
An unfair action is not right or fair.

point out idiom 지적하다
If you point out a fact or mistake, you tell someone about it or draw their attention to it.

literally [lítərəli] ad. 그야말로
You use literally to emphasize that what you are saying is true, even though it seems exaggerated or surprising.

challenge [ʧǽlindʒ] n. 도전
A challenge is something new and difficult which requires great effort and determination.

windshield [wíndʃì:ld] n. (자동차 등의) 앞유리
The windshield of a car or other vehicle is the glass window at the front through which the driver looks.

sniffle [snifl] v. 훌쩍거리다
When someone sniffles, they make soft, quiet sounds, usually because they are crying.

statue [stǽʧuː] n. 조각상
A statue is a large sculpture of a person or an animal, made of stone or metal.

unmoved [ənmúvd] a. 냉정한
If you are unmoved by something, you are not emotionally affected by it.

deathbed [déθbèd] n. 임종(의 자리)
If someone is on their deathbed, they are in a bed and about to die.

league [liːg] n. 수준
You use the word league to make comparisons between different people or things, especially in terms of their quality.

scared [skɛərd] a. 무서워하는, 겁먹은
If you are scared of someone or something, you are frightened of them.

hold back idiom 참다, 억제하다
If you hold back something such as tears or laughter, or if you hold back, you make an effort to stop yourself from showing how you feel.

realize [ríːəlàiz] v. 인식하다, 자각하다
If you realize something, you become aware of it, understand it, or accept it after thinking about it or discovering it.

approach [əpróuʧ] n. 접근 방법
Your approach to a task, problem, or situation is the way you deal with it or think about it.

drown [draun] v. 물에 빠지다
When someone drowns or is drowned, they die because they have gone or been pushed under water and cannot breathe.

shed [ʃed] v. (빛을) 비추다
If something sheds light, it lights the area around it.

startle [staːrtl] v. 깜짝 놀라게 하다
If something sudden and unexpected startles you, it surprises and frightens you slightly.

lava [láːvə] n. 용암
Lava is the very hot liquid rock that comes out of a volcano.

cheek [ʧiːk] n. 뺨, 볼
Your cheeks are the sides of your face below your eyes.

land [lænd] v. (땅·표면에) 떨어지다
When someone or something lands, they come down to the ground after moving through the air or falling.

hiss [his] n. 쉬익 하는 소리
A hiss is a sound like a long 's'.

Check Your Reading Speed

1분에 몇 단어를 읽는지 리딩 속도를 측정해 보세요.

$$\frac{1{,}711 \text{ words}}{\text{reading time (}\quad\text{) sec}} \times 60 = (\quad) \text{ WPM}$$

Build Your Vocabulary

repair [ripέər] v. 수리하다
If you repair something that has been damaged or is not working properly, you fix it.

punch [pʌntʃ] v. 주먹으로 치다
If you punch someone or something, you hit them hard with your fist.

disappear [disəpíər] v. 사라지다
When someone or something disappears, you can no longer see them.

hammer [hǽmər] n. 망치
A hammer is a tool that consists of a heavy piece of metal at the end of a handle.

swallow [swálou] v. 마른침을 삼키다
If you swallow, you make a movement in your throat as if you are swallowing something, often because you are nervous or frightened.

solid [sálid] a. 단단한
Solid means firm, strong, or not easily broken.

ticket [tíkit] n. (벌금을 부과하는) 딱지
A ticket is an official piece of paper which orders you to pay a fine or to appear in court because you have committed a driving or parking offence.

hang up idiom 전화를 끊다
If you hang up or you hang up the phone, you end a phone call.

teary [tíəri] a. 눈물이 글썽한
When your eyes are teary, they are moist or shiny as if you are about to cry.

incredulously [inkrédʒuləsli] ad. 의심하는 듯이
Incredulously means in a way that shows you cannot believe something.

approach [əpróutʃ] v. 다가가다, 접근하다
To approach something means to get closer to it.

pitcher [pítʃər] n. 물 주전자
A pitcher is a container for holding and pouring out liquids.

talent [tǽlənt] n. 재능
Talent is the natural ability to do something well.

slip [slip] v. 슬며시 가다
If you slip somewhere, you go there quickly and quietly.

opportunity [àpərtjú:nəti] n. 기회
An opportunity is a situation in which it is possible for you to do something that you want to do.

glow [glou] v. 빛나다
When something glows, it produces a steady light.

incredible [inkrédəbl] a. 굉장한
If you say that something is incredible, you mean that it is very unusual or surprising, and you cannot believe it is really true, although it may be.

gush [gʌʃ] v. 마구 표현하다
If someone gushes, they express their admiration or pleasure in an exaggerated way.

nervously [nə́:rvəsli] ad. 초조하게
If you do something nervously, you do it while feeling worried or not relaxed.

walk [wɔ:k] v. (걸어서) 바래다주다
If you walk someone somewhere, you walk there with them in order to show politeness or to make sure that they get there safely.

spar [spa:r] v. 옥신각신하다
If you spar with someone, you argue with them but not in an aggressive or serious way.

fiery [fáiəri] a. 불의, 화염의
If you describe something as fiery, you mean that it is burning strongly or contains fire.

catch one's breath idiom 한숨 돌리다
When you catch your breath while you are doing something energetic, you stop for a short time so that you can start breathing normally again.

huff and puff idiom (몹시 지쳐서) 헉헉거리다
If someone huffs and puffs, they breathe in a noisy way because you are very tired.

gasp [gæsp] v. 헉 하고 숨을 쉬다
When you gasp, you take a short quick breath through your mouth, especially when you are surprised or shocked.

throw up idiom 토하다, 게우다
When someone throws up, they vomit.

dizzy [dízi] a. 어지러운
If you feel dizzy, you feel that you are losing your balance and are about to fall.

stagger [stǽgər] v. 비틀거리다
If you stagger, you walk very unsteadily, for example because you are ill.

bush [buʃ] n. 관목, 덤불
A bush is a large plant which is smaller than a tree and has a lot of branches.

race [reis] v. 급히 가다
If you race somewhere, you go there as quickly as possible.

groan [groun] v. (고통·짜증으로) 신음 소리를 내다
If you groan something, you say it in a low, unhappy voice.

sarcastically [sa:rkǽstikəli] ad. 비꼬는 투로
If you say something sarcastically, you say the opposite of what you mean, in order to make an unkind joke or to show that you are annoyed.

faraway [fɑ́:rəwei] a. 멀리 떨어진
A faraway place is a long distance from you or from a particular place.

roil [rɔil] v. 요동치다
To roil means to move quickly in a twisting circular movement.

hop [hap] v. 급히 움직이다
If you hop somewhere, you move there quickly or suddenly.

rev [rev] v. (엔진의) 회전 속도를 올리다
When you rev a vehicle, the engine speed is increased.

zip [zip] v. 쌩 하고 가다
If you say that something or someone zips somewhere, you mean that they move there very quickly.

for dear life idiom 죽어라고, 필사적으로
If you run, fight, or hold on for dear life, you do it as fast or as well as you can because you are afraid.

regain [rigéin] v. 되찾다
If you regain something that you have lost, you get it back again.

in time idiom 시간 맞춰, 늦지 않게
If you are in time for a particular event, you are not too late for it.

exclaim [ikskléim] v. 외치다
If you exclaim, you cry out suddenly in surprise, strong emotion, or pain.

yell [jel] v. 소리치다
If you yell, you shout loudly, usually because you are excited, angry, or in pain.

growl [graul] v. 으르렁거리듯 말하다
If someone growls something, they say something in a low, rough, and angry voice.

weave [wi:v] v. 이리저리 빠져 나가다
If you weave your way somewhere, you move between and around things as you go there.

traffic [træfik] n. 차량들, 교통(량)
Traffic refers to all the vehicles that are moving along the roads in a particular area.

stretch [stretʃ] v. 늘어나다
When something soft or elastic stretches or is stretched, it becomes longer or bigger as well as thinner, usually because it is pulled.

insist [insíst] v. 우기다, 고집하다
To insist means to demand that something must be done or that you must have a particular thing.

gesture [dʒéstʃər] v. 가리키다, 몸짓을 하다
If you gesture, you use movements of your hands or head in order to tell someone something or draw their attention to something.

swerve [swə:rv] v. 방향을 바꾸다
If a vehicle or other moving thing swerves or if you swerve it, it suddenly changes direction, often in order to avoid hitting something.

ripple [ripl] v. 잔물결을 일으키다
When the wind ripples plants or trees or when they ripple, they move in a wave-like motion.

skid [skid] v. 미끄러지다
If something skids, it slides suddenly while moving, usually sideways.

slosh [slaʃ] v. 철벅거리다
If a liquid sloshes around, it moves in a noisy or messy way.

flicker [flíkər] v. (불·빛 등이) 깜박거리다
If a light or flame flickers, it shines unsteadily.

trap [træp] v. 가두다
When you're trapped, it means something is stopping you from going where you want to go.

fill someone's shoes idiom ~을 대신해서 그런대로 일을 해내다
If you fill someone's shoes, you do their job in an acceptable way when they are not there.

sigh [sai] v. 한숨을 쉬다
When you sigh, you let out a deep breath, as a way of expressing feelings such as disappointment, tiredness, or pleasure.

repay [ripéi] v. 보답하다
If you repay a favor that someone did for you, you do something for them in return.

sacrifice [sǽkrəfais] n. 희생
A sacrifice is the act of giving up something that is valuable to you in order to help someone else.

descend [disénd] v. 내려가다
If you descend or if you descend a staircase, you move downward from a higher to a lower level.

nearby [nìərbái] a. 바로 가까이의
If something is nearby, it is only a short distance away.

platform [plǽtfɔːrm] n. (역의) 승강장
A platform in a railway station is the area beside the rails where you wait for or get off a train.

mutter [mʌ́tər] v. 중얼거리다
If you mutter, you speak very quietly so that you cannot easily be heard, often because you are complaining about something.

freeze [fri:z] v. (froze-frozen) (두려움 등으로 몸이) 얼어붙다
If someone who is moving freezes, they suddenly stop and become completely still and quiet.

take a breath idiom 심호흡을 하다
If you say that you took a breath before doing something dangerous or frightening, you mean that you tried to make yourself feel strong and confident.

silence [sáiləns] int. 조용히 해!, 쉿!
Silence is used to tell people to be quiet.

stink [stiŋk] v. 냄새가 나다
To stink means to smell extremely unpleasant.

flame [fleim] v. (얼굴이) 새빨개지다
If someone's face flames, it suddenly looks red, usually because they are angry.

sniff [snif] v. 냄새를 맡다
If you sniff something, you breathe air in through the nose in order to discover or enjoy the smell of it.

dawn [dɔ:n] v. 분명해지다
If a fact or idea dawns on you, you realize it.

matchmaking [mǽtʃmèikiŋ] n. 결혼 중매
Matchmaking is the activity of encouraging people you know to form relationships or get married.

surface [sə́:rfis] n. 표면
When you refer to the surface of a situation, you are talking about what can be seen easily rather than what is hidden or not immediately obvious.

forcefully [fɔ́:rsfəli] ad. 강하게
If you do something forcefully, you do it in a way that uses force.

flinch [flinʧ] v. 움찔하다
If you flinch, you make a small sudden movement, especially when something surprises you or hurts you.

pleasant [plézənt] a. 쾌적한, 즐거운
Something that is pleasant is nice, enjoyable, or attractive.

sensation [senséiʃən] n. 느낌
A sensation is a physical feeling.

flaming [fléimiŋ] a. 불타는
Flaming describes something that is burning or on fire.

gulp [gʌlp] v. 침을 꿀꺽 삼키다; n. 꿀꺽 삼키기
If you gulp, you swallow air, often making a noise in your throat as you do so, because you are nervous or excited.

thoughtfully [θɔ́:tfəli] ad. 생각에 잠겨
If you say something thoughtfully, you say it in a way that shows you are thinking a lot about something.

whisper [hwíspər] v. 속삭이다
When you whisper, you say something very quietly, using your breath rather than your throat, so that only one person can hear you.

refract [rifrǽkt] v. 굴절시키다
When a ray of light or a sound wave refracts or is refracted, the path it follows bends at a particular point, for example when it enters water or glass.

magnifying glass [mǽgnəfàiiŋ glæs] n. 돋보기
A magnifying glass is a piece of glass which makes objects appear bigger than they actually are.

beam [bi:m] n. 광선
A beam is a line of energy, radiation, or particles sent in a particular direction.

burst [bə:rst] v. 갑자기 ~하다
If you burst into tears, laughter, or song, you suddenly begin to cry, laugh, or sing.

blink [bliŋk] v. 눈을 깜박이다
When you blink or when you blink your eyes, you shut your eyes and very quickly open them again.

intermingle [intərmíŋgl] v. 섞이다
If things intermingle, they mix together.

horrified [hɔ́:rəfàid] a. 겁에 질린
If someone is horrified, they feel shocked or disgusted, usually because of something that they have seen or heard.

rush [rʌʃ] v. 급히 보내다
If you rush someone or something to a place, you take them there quickly.

match [mætʃ] n. 어울리는 사람
If a combination of things or people is a good match, they have a pleasing effect when placed or used together.

yelp [jelp] v. 비명을 지르다
If a person or dog yelps, they give a sudden short cry, often because of fear or pain.

reluctantly [rilʌ́ktəntli] ad. 마지못해
If you do something reluctantly, you do it even though you do not really want to.

dart [da:rt] v. 휙 눈길을 던지다
If you dart a look at someone or something, or if your eyes dart to them, you look at them very quickly.

reopening [rióupəniŋ] n. 재개장
A reopening is the act of opening again something that was closed.

clap [klæp] v. 박수를 치다
When you clap, you hit your hands together to show appreciation or attract attention.

overjoyed [òuvərdʒɔ́id] a. 매우 기뻐하는
If you are overjoyed, you are extremely pleased about something.

counter [káuntər] n. 계산대
In a place such as a shop or café, a counter is a long narrow table or flat surface at which customers are served.

recall [rikɔ́:l] v. 상기하다
If you recall something, you bring it back into your mind and remember it.

board [bɔ:rd] v. 탑승하다
When you board a train, ship, or aircraft, you get on it in order to travel somewhere.

respect [rispékt] n. 존경, 경의
If you have respect for someone, you have a good opinion of them.

blessing [blésiŋ] n. 축복
A blessing is something good that you are grateful for.

burden [bə́:rdn] n. 짐, 부담
If you describe a problem or a responsibility as a burden, you mean that it causes someone a lot of difficulty, worry, or hard work.

well [wel] v. (액체가) 솟아 나오다
If liquids, for example tears, well, they come to the surface and form a pool.

ELEMENTAL

package [pǽkidʒ] n. 소포
A package is an object or group of objects wrapped in paper or packed in a box.

reveal [rivíːl] v. 드러내 보이다
To reveal something means to make people aware of it.

stunned [stʌnd] a. 깜짝 놀란
If you are stunned by something, you are extremely shocked or surprised by it and are therefore unable to speak or do anything.

flare [flɛər] v. 확 타오르다
When a fire flares up, it suddenly burns more intensely.

youthful [júːθfəl] a. 젊은
Someone who is youthful behaves as if they are young or younger than they really are.

unveil [ʌnvéil] v. (새로운 상품 등을) 발표하다
If you unveil a plan, new product, or some other thing that has been kept secret, you introduce it to the public.

chuckle [ʧʌkl] v. 빙그레 웃다
When you chuckle, you laugh quietly.

exhaust [igzɔ́ːst] v. 기진맥진하게 만들다
If something exhausts you, it makes you so tired, either physically or mentally, that you have no energy left.

shoot [ʃuːt] v. (shot-shot) (눈길 등을) 휙 던지다
If you shoot a look at someone, you look at them quickly and briefly, often in a way that expresses your feelings.

dim [dim] v. 희미해지다
If a light dims, it becomes less bright.

pressure [préʃər] n. 압력
The pressure in a place or container is the force produced by the quantity of gas or liquid in that place or container.

immense [iméns] a. 엄청난
If you describe something as immense, you mean that it is extremely large or great.

tiny [táini] a. 아주 작은
Tiny describes something that is very small in size or extent.

15 & 16

1. Why did Wade take Ember Garden Central Station?

    A. To get on a train

    B. To explore the abandoned place

    C. To let her spend time with Gale

    D. To show the Vivisteria flower to her

2. Why was Ember in a protective bubble?

    A. To test the strength of Gale's blow

    B. To breathe underwater

    C. To be invisible

    D. To stay warm

3. **What did Wade and Ember do after their hands touched each other?**
   A. They began to dance.
   B. They ran away to another town.
   C. They started to cry.
   D. They hurried to share the news.

4. **Why did Bernie close the shop for a few days?**
   A. To have a vacation
   B. To repair the shop
   C. To prepare for a party
   D. To get enough rest

5. **What did Bernie do when he realized Ember caused the leak in the shop?**
   A. He retired from the shop.
   B. He got on his scooter to leave.
   C. He quietly left the stage.
   D. He decided not to retire anymore.

Check Your Reading Speed
1분에 몇 단어를 읽는지 리딩 속도를 측정해 보세요.

$$\frac{1,647 \text{ words}}{\text{reading time ( ) sec}} \times 60 = (\quad) \text{ WPM}$$

Build Your Vocabulary

thrilled [θrild] a. 아주 신이 난
If someone is thrilled, they are extremely pleased about something.

gently [dʒéntli] ad. 부드럽게
Gently means in a kind, mild, or careful manner.

stare [stɛər] v. 빤히 쳐다보다
If you stare at someone or something, you look at them for a long time.

mesmerize [mézməràiz] v. 마음을 사로잡다
If you are mesmerized by something, you are so interested in it or so attracted to it that you cannot think about anything else.

murmur [mə́:rmə] v. 중얼거리다
If you murmur something, you say it very quietly so that not many people can hear what you are saying.

expression [ikspréʃən] n. 표정
Your expression is the way that your face looks at a particular moment.

boot [bu:t] n. 목이 긴 신발, 부츠
Boots are shoes that cover your whole foot and the lower part of your leg.

deserted [dizə́:rtid] a. 버림받은
If a place is deserted, there are no people in it.

faded [féidid] a. 색이 바랜
A faded object is less colorful than previously.

advertise [ǽdvərtàiz] v. 광고하다
If you advertise something such as a product, an event, or a job, you tell people about it online, in newspapers, on television, or on posters in order to encourage them to buy the product, go to the event, or apply for the job.

banner [bǽnər] n. 현수막
A banner is a long strip of cloth with something written on it.

exhibit [igzíbit] n. 전시
An exhibit is a public display of paintings, sculpture, or objects of interest, for example in a museum or art gallery.

melt [melt] v. 녹이다
When a solid substance melts or when you melt it, it changes to a liquid, usually because it has been heated.

entryway [éntriwèi] n. 입구의 통로
An entryway is a passage that is used as an entrance to a building.

knock [nak] v. (움직이도록) 치다
If you knock something, you touch or hit it roughly, especially so that it falls or moves.

ornate [ɔːrnéit] a. 화려하게 장식된
An ornate building, piece of furniture, or object is decorated with complicated patterns or shapes.

drip [drip] v. 떨어지다
When liquid drips somewhere, or you drip it somewhere, it falls in individual small drops.

ceiling [síːliŋ] n. 천장
A ceiling is the horizontal surface that forms the top part or roof inside a room.

vanish [vǽniʃ] v. 사라지다
If someone or something vanishes, they disappear suddenly or in a way that cannot be explained.

flooded [flʌ́did] a. 물에 잠긴
If a place is flooded, it becomes covered in water.

puzzled [pʌ́zld] a. 어리둥절해하는
Someone who is puzzled is confused because they do not understand something.

signal [sígnəl] n. 신호
A signal is a gesture, sound, or action which is intended to give a particular message to the person who sees or hears it.

inhale [inhéil] v. 숨을 들이마시다
When you inhale, you breathe in.

surface [sə́ːrfis] n. 표면
Surface is the flat top part or the outside of something.

stunned [stʌnd] a. 깜짝 놀란
If you are stunned by something, you are extremely shocked or surprised by it and are therefore unable to speak or do anything.

brow [brau] n. 이마
Your brow is your forehead.

furrow [fə́ːrou] v. (미간이) 찡그러지다
If someone furrows their brow or forehead or if it furrows, deep folds appear in it because the person is annoyed, unhappy, or confused.

edge [edʒ] n. 가장자리
The edge of something is the place or line where it stops, or the part of it that is furthest from the middle.

seal [siːl] v. 밀폐하다, 틈을 막다
If you seal a container or an opening, you cover it with something in order to prevent air, liquid, or other material getting in or out.

leak [liːk] v. (액체·기체가) 새다
If a liquid or gas leaks, it escapes through a hole or crack.

steady [stédi] v. 균형을 잡다; ad. 안정되게; a. 흔들림 없는
If you steady something or if it steadies, it stops shaking or moving about.

grab [græb] v. 움켜잡다
If you grab something, you take it or pick it up suddenly and roughly.

protective [prətéktiv] a. 보호용의
Something that is protective is designed to protect or shield from harm, damage, or injury.

illuminate [ilúːmənèit] v. 비추다
To illuminate something means to shine light on it and to make it brighter and more visible.

gorgeous [gɔ́ːrdʒəs] a. 아주 멋진
If you say that something is gorgeous, you mean that it gives you a lot of pleasure or is very attractive.

preserve [prizə́:rv] v. 보존하다
If you preserve something, you take action to save it or protect it from damage or decay.

vaulted [vɔ́:ltid] a. 아치형의, 둥근 천장의
A vaulted thing is made in the shape of an arch or a series of arches or has a ceiling or roof of this shape.

crisscross [krískrɔ̀:s] v. 교차하다
To crisscross means to make a pattern on something with many straight lines that cross each other.

explore [iksplɔ́:r] v. 탐험하다
If you explore a place, you go around it where you have never been in order to find out what is there.

startle [sta:rtl] v. 깜짝 놀라게 하다
If something sudden and unexpected startles you, it surprises and frightens you slightly.

school [sku:l] n. (물고기 등의) 떼, 무리
A school of fish or dolphins is a large group of them moving through water together.

swirl [swə:rl] v. 빙빙 돌다
If you swirl something liquid or flowing, or if it swirls, it moves round and round quickly.

grand [grænd] a. 웅장한
If you describe a building or a piece of scenery as grand, you mean that its size or appearance is very impressive.

ballroom [bɔ́:lru:m] n. 무도회장
A ballroom is a very large room that is used for dancing.

dormant [dɔ́:rmənt] a. 성장을 중단한
Something that is dormant is not active, growing, or being used at the present time but is capable of becoming active later on.

vine [vain] n. 덩굴 식물
A vine is a plant that grows up or over things, especially one which produces grapes.

bloom [blu:m] v. 꽃이 피다
If a plant blooms, its flowers open.

purplish [pə́:rpliʃ] a. 자줏빛을 띤
Purplish means slightly purple in color.

light up idiom 환해지다
If your face or your eyes light up, you suddenly look very surprised or happy.

explode [iksplóud] v. 폭발적으로 증가하다
If something explodes, it increases suddenly and rapidly in number or intensity.

shrink [ʃriŋk] v. 줄어들다
If something shrinks or something else shrinks it, it becomes smaller.

run out idiom 다 써 버리다
If you run out of something, you have no more of it left.

frantically [frǽntikəli] ad. 미친 듯이
If you do something frantically, you behave in a wild and uncontrolled way because you are frightened or worried.

stairwell [stέərwèl] n. 계단이 나 있는 공간
The stairwell is the part of a building that contains the staircase.

tighten [taitn] v. 꽉 죄다
To tighten means to make something or become more difficult to move, open or separate.

pant [pænt] v. (숨을) 헐떡이다
If you pant, you breathe quickly and loudly with your mouth open, usually because you have been doing something energetic.

strength [streŋkθ] n. 힘
Your strength is the physical energy that you have, which gives you the ability to perform various actions, such as lifting or moving things.

in time idiom 시간 맞춰, 늦지 않게
If you are in time for a particular event, you are not too late for it.

land [lænd] v. (땅·표면에) 떨어지다
When someone or something lands, they come down to the ground after moving through the air or falling.

sidewalk [sáidwɔːk] n. 보도
A sidewalk is a paved path for pedestrians beside a road.

collapse [kəlǽps] v. 쓰러지다
If you collapse, you suddenly faint or fall down because you are very ill or weak.

side by side idiom 나란히
If two people or things are side by side, they are next to each other.

regret [rigrét] n. 후회
Regret is a feeling of sadness or disappointment, which is caused by something that has happened or something that you have done or not done.

spring [spriŋ] v. (sprang-sprang) 휙 움직이다
If someone or something springs in a particular direction, it moves suddenly and quickly.

inspiring [inspáiəriŋ] a. 영감을 주는
Something or someone that is inspiring is exciting and makes you feel strongly interested and enthusiastic.

prove [pruːv] v. 입증하다, 증명하다
If you prove that something is true, you show by means of argument or evidence that it is definitely true.

plead [pliːd] v. 애원하다
If you plead with someone to do something, you ask them in an intense, emotional way to do it.

disaster [dizǽstər] n. 엄청난 불행, 재앙
If you refer to something as a disaster, you are emphasizing that you think it is extremely bad or unacceptable.

remind [rimáind] v. 상기시키다
If someone reminds you of a fact or event that you already know about, they say something which makes you think about it.

vaporize [véipəràiz] v. 증발시키다
If a liquid or solid vaporizes or if you vaporize it, it changes into vapor or gas.

extinguish [ikstíŋgwiʃ] v. (불을) 끄다
If you extinguish a fire or a light, you stop it burning or shining.

cut off idiom (말을) 중단시키다
If you cut someone off, you interrupt them when they are speaking.

tentatively [téntətivli] ad. 망설이며
When you do something tentatively, you do it in a way that is not done with confidence.

hover [hʌ́vər] v. 맴돌다
To hover means to stay in the same position in the air without moving forward or backward.

yank [jæŋk] v. 홱 잡아당기다
If you yank someone or something somewhere, you pull them there suddenly and with a lot of force.

palm [pɑːm] n. 손바닥
The palm of your hand is the inside part of your hand, between your fingers and your wrist.

steam [stiːm] n. 증기
Steam is the gas that water produces when you heat it.

hiss [his] v. 쉬익 하는 소리를 내다
To hiss means to make a sound like a long 's'.

examine [igzǽmin] v. 조사하다
If you examine something, you look at it carefully.

amazed [əméizd] a. 놀란
If you are amazed, you are very surprised.

firmly [fɔ́ːrmli] ad. 확고하게
If you do something firmly, you do it in a strong or definite way.

tingle [tiŋgl] v. 따끔거리다
When a part of your body tingles, you have a slight stinging feeling there.

interlock [intərlák] v. 서로 맞물리게 하다
Things that interlock or are interlocked go between or through each other so that they are linked.

equilibrium [ìːkwəlíbriəm] n. 균형
Equilibrium is a balance between several different influences or aspects of a situation.

chemistry [kéməstri] n. 화학적 성질
The chemistry of an organism or a material is the chemical substances that make it up and the chemical reactions that go on inside it.

lean [liːn] v. (몸을) 숙이다
When you lean in a particular direction, you bend your body in that direction.

spark [spɑːrk] v. 촉발시키다
If one thing sparks another, the first thing causes the second thing to start happening.

picture [píkʧər] v. (마음속에) 그리다
If you picture something in your mind, you think of it and have such a clear idea of it that you seem to be able to see it.

exhausted [igzɔ́:stid] a. 기진맥진한
If you are exhausted, you are very tired.

flash [flæʃ] v. 번쩍이다
If a light flashes or if you flash a light, it shines with a sudden bright light, especially as quick, regular flashes of light.

vulnerable [vʌ́lnərəbl] a. 약한
Something that is vulnerable can be easily harmed or affected by something bad.

confusion [kənfjú:ʒən] n. (정신 상태의) 혼란
If your mind is in a state of confusion, you do not know what to believe or what you should do.

take over idiom ~을 이어받다
If you take over a company, you get control of it.

opportunity [àpərtjú:nəti] n. 기회
An opportunity is a situation in which it is possible for you to do something that you want to do.

whirl [hwə:rl] v. 빙빙 돌다
When you whirl, you turn or spin around rapidly.

platform [plǽtfɔ:rm] n. (역의) 승강장
A platform in a railway station is the area beside the rails where you wait for or get off a train.

repeat [ripí:t] v. 한 번 더 말하다
If you repeat something, you say or write it again.

luxury [lʌ́kʃəri] n. 사치, 호사
A luxury is something expensive which is not necessary but which gives you pleasure.

absolutely [æbsəlú:tli] ad. 전혀
Absolutely is used to emphasize something negative.

set one's jaw idiom 이를 악물다
To set your jaw means to move your lower jaw forward in a way that shows your determination.

ignite [ignáit] v. 점화하다
When you ignite something or when it ignites, it starts burning or explodes.

don't you dare idiom 감히 ~할 생각 마!
If you say to someone 'don't you dare' do something, you are telling them not to do it and letting them know that you are angry.

give up idiom 포기하다
If you give up, you decide that you cannot do something and stop trying to do it.

glower [gláuər] v. 찡그리다
If you glower at someone or something, you look at them angrily.

shaky [ʃéiki] a. 떨리는
If your body or your voice is shaky, you cannot control it properly and it shakes, for example because you are ill or nervous.

hold back idiom 참다, 억제하다
If you hold back something such as tears or laughter, or if you hold back, you make an effort to stop yourself from showing how you feel.

Check Your Reading Speed

1분에 몇 단어를 읽는지 리딩 속도를 측정해 보세요.

$$\frac{1{,}193 \text{ words}}{\text{reading time (} \quad \text{) sec}} \times 60 = (\quad) \text{ WPM}$$

Build Your Vocabulary

grand [grænd] a. 화려한
If you describe an activity or experience as grand, you mean that it is very pleasant and enjoyable.

reopening [rióupəniŋ] n. 재개장
A reopening is the act of opening again something that was closed.

community [kəmjú:nəti] n. 주민, 지역 사회
The community is all the people who live in a particular area or place.

gather [gǽðər] v. 모이다
If people gather somewhere or if someone gathers people somewhere, they come together in a group.

outdoor [áutdɔ̀:r] a. 야외의
Outdoor activities or things happen or are used outside and not in a building.

snack [snæk] v. 간단히 식사를 하다
If you snack, you eat snacks between or instead of main meals.

ceremonial [sèrəmóuniəl] a. 의식용의
Something that is ceremonial relates to a ceremony or is used in a ceremony.

flame [fleim] n. 불꽃
A flame is the hot, bright, and burning gas produced by something on fire.

pedestal [pédəstl] n. 받침대
A pedestal is the base on which something such as a statue stands.

nearby [nìərbái] a. 바로 가까이의
If something is nearby, it is only a short distance away.

honored [ánərd] a. 영광으로 생각하는
If you are honored to do something, you are proud that you have been given special respect or a special opportunity.

serve [sə:rv] v. ~을 위해 일하다
If you serve your country, an organization, or a person, you do useful work for them.

affectionately [əfékʃənətli] ad. 애정을 담아
If you do something affectionately, you do it in a way that shows caring feelings and love for someone.

take over idiom ~을 이어받다
If you take over a company, you get control of it.

ablaze [əbléiz] a. 불길에 휩싸인
Something that is ablaze is burning very fiercely.

clear [kliər] v. (연기 등이) 걷히다
When fog or mist clears, it slowly disappears.

glory [glɔ́:ri] n. 영광
Glory is the fame and admiration that you gain by doing something impressive.

audience [ɔ́:diəns] n. 관중, 관객
The audience at a play, concert, film, or public meeting is the group of people watching or listening to it.

cheer [ʧiər] v. 환호하다
When people cheer, they shout loudly to show their approval or to encourage someone who is doing something such as taking part in a game.

trick [trik] n. 비결, 요령
A trick is a clever way of doing something.

hesitate [hézətèit] v. 망설이다, 주저하다
If you hesitate, you do not speak or act for a short time, usually because you are uncertain, embarrassed, or worried about what you are going to say or do.

weight [weit] n. (무거운 책임감 같은) 짐, 부담
The weight of something is a great responsibility or worry.

swallow [swálou] v. 마른침을 삼키다; (음식 등을) 삼키다
If you swallow, you make a movement in your throat as if you are swallowing something, often because you are nervous or frightened.

bunch [bʌntʃ] n. 다발, 묶음
A bunch of things is a number of things, especially a large number.

element [éləmənt] n. 원소
An element is one of the four substances (earth, air, fire, and water) from which people used to believe that everything was made.

nod [nad] v. (고개를) 끄덕이다
If you nod, you move your head up and down to show agreement, understanding, or approval.

agreement [əgríːmənt] n. 동의
Agreement with someone means having the same opinion as they have.

fib [fib] v. 거짓말을 하다
If someone is fibbing, they are telling lies.

unconvincingly [ʌnkənvínsiŋli] ad. 설득력 없이
When you do something unconvincingly, you do it in a way that does not make you believe that something is true.

crash [kræʃ] v. (파티에) 초대도 받지 않고 가다, 쳐들어가다
If you crash one's party, you go to the party that you have not been invited to.

admit [ædmít] v. 인정하다
If you admit something, you agree, often unwillingly, that it is true.

demonstrate [démənstrèit] v. (행동으로) 보여 주다
If you demonstrate a particular skill, quality, or feeling, you show by your actions that you have it.

mug [mʌg] n. (큰) 잔, 머그잔
A mug is a large deep cup with straight sides and a handle, used for hot drinks.

content [kántent] n. 내용물
The contents of a container such as a bottle, box, or room are the things that are inside it.

strain [strein] v. 안간힘을 쓰다
If you strain to do something, you make a great effort to do it when it is difficult to do.

unpleasant [ʌnplézənt] a. 불쾌한
If something is unpleasant, it gives you bad feelings, for example by making you feel upset or uncomfortable.

croak [krouk] v. 목이 쉰 듯 말하다
If someone croaks something, they say it in a low, rough voice.

recognize [rékəgnàiz] v. 알아보다
If you recognize someone or something, you know who that person is or what that thing is.

inspector [inspéktər] n. 조사관
An inspector is a person, usually employed by a government agency, whose job is to find out whether people are obeying official regulations.

ban [bæn] v. 금지하다
To ban something means to state officially that it must not be done, shown, or used.

impossible [impásəbl] a. 불가능한
Something that is impossible cannot be done or cannot happen.

chemistry [kéməstri] n. 화학적 성질
The chemistry of an organism or a material is the chemical substances that make it up and the chemical reactions that go on inside it.

gaze [geiz] v. 응시하다, 바라보다
To gaze at something or someone means to look steadily and intently, especially in admiration, surprise, or thought.

exasperated [igzǽspərèitid] a. 몹시 화가 난
If you describe a person as exasperated, you mean that they are frustrated or angry because of something that is happening or something that another person is doing.

inspection [inspékʃən] n. 점검, 검사
An inspection is the act of looking closely at someone or something, especially to check that everything is as it should be.

stand one's ground idiom 자기 주장을 고집하다
If you stand your ground, you do not run away from a situation, but face it bravely.

jab [dʒæb] v. 찌르다
If you jab one thing into another, you push it there with a quick, sudden movement and with a lot of force.

fiery [fáiəri] a. 불의, 화염의
If you describe something as fiery, you mean that it is burning strongly or contains fire.

flooded [flʌ́did] a. 물에 잠긴
If a place is flooded, it becomes covered in water.

basement [béismənt] n. 지하실
A basement of a building is a room or floor that is built partly or entirely below ground level.

accuse [əkjúːz] v. 비난하다
If you accuse someone of doing something wrong or dishonest, you say or tell them that you believe that they did it.

involuntarily [inváləntèrəli] ad. 본의 아니게
If you do something involuntarily, you do it without you intending it or being able to control it.

dart [daːrt] v. 휙 눈길을 던지다
If you dart a look at someone or something, or if your eyes dart to them, you look at them very quickly.

widen [waidn] v. (놀람 등으로) 둥그레지다
If your eyes widen, they open more.

damage [dǽmidʒ] n. 손상, 피해
Damage consists of the unpleasant effects that something has on a person, situation, or type of activity.

narrow [nǽrou] v. (눈이) 찌푸려지다
If your eyes narrow or if you narrow your eyes, you almost close them, for example because you are angry or because you are trying to concentrate on something.

stammer [stǽmər] v. 말을 더듬다
If you stammer, you speak with difficulty, hesitating and repeating words or sounds.

bellow [bélou] v. 고함치다
To bellow means to shout in a deep, loud voice.

speechless [spíːʃlis] a. (강한 감정 때문에) 말을 못 하는
If you are speechless, you are temporarily unable to speak, usually because something has shocked you.

embrace [imbréis] v. 받아들이다
If you embrace a change, political system, or idea, you accept it and start supporting it or believing in it.

recite [risáit] v. 죽 말하다
If you recite something such as a list, you say it aloud.

be torn idiom 갈피를 잡지 못하다
If you are torn between two or more things, you cannot decide which to choose, and so you feel anxious or troubled.

flatly [flǽtli] ad. 단호하게
If you say something flatly, you say it in a way that is very definite and will not be changed.

culvert [kʌ́lvərt] n. 지하 배수로
A culvert is a tunnel that carries water under a road.

confess [kənfés] v. 고백하다, 인정하다
If you confess something, you admit something that you feel embarrassed about.

protest [prətést] v. 이의를 제기하듯이 말하다
If you protest that something is the case, you insist that it is the case, when other people think that it may not be.

holler [hálər] v. 소리지르다, 고함치다
If you holler, you shout loudly.

slice [slais] v. 가르다
If something slices through a substance, it moves through it quickly, like a knife.

spray [sprei] v. 분사하다, 분무하다
If you spray a liquid somewhere or if it sprays somewhere, drops of the liquid cover a place or shower someone.

heartbroken [háːrtbròukən] a. 비통해하는
Someone who is heartbroken is very sad and emotionally upset.

sag [sæg] v. 축 처지다
When part of someone's body begins to sag, it starts to become less firm and hang down.

glare [glɛər] v. 노려보다
When you glare at someone, you look at them with an angry expression on your face.

betrayal [bitréiəl] n. 배신
A betrayal is an action which hurt someone who trust you, especially by lying to or about them or telling their secret to other people.

flicker [flíkər] v. 스치다
If an emotion or expression flickers on someone's face or through their mind, it exists or is shown for only a short time.

shame [ʃeim] n. 수치심
Shame is an uncomfortable feeling that you get when you have done something wrong or embarrassing.

cough [kɔːf] v. 기침하다
When you cough, you force air out of your throat with a sudden, harsh noise.

retire [ritáiər] v. 은퇴하다
When people retire, they leave their job and usually stop working completely.

storm [stɔːrm] v. 쿵쾅대며 가다
If you storm into or out of a place, you enter or leave it quickly and noisily, because you are angry.

subdued [səbdjúːd] a. 약해진
Subdued lights or colors are not very bright.

disappear [disəpíər] v. 사라지다
When someone or something disappears, you can no longer see them.

dusk [dʌsk] n. 황혼, 땅거미
Dusk is the time just before night when the daylight has almost gone but when it is not completely dark.

consume [kənsúːm] v. (강렬한 감정이) 사로잡다
If a feeling or idea consumes you, it affects you very strongly indeed.

in the distance idiom 저 멀리, 먼 곳에 (= into the distance)
If you can see something in the distance, you can see it, far away from you.

sigh [sai] v. 한숨을 쉬다
When you sigh, you let out a deep breath, as a way of expressing feelings such as disappointment, tiredness, or pleasure.

aloud [əláud] ad. 큰 소리로
When you say something, read, or laugh aloud, you speak or laugh so that other people can hear you.

frustration [frʌstréiʃən] n. 좌질감
Frustration is a feeling you get when you can't do or get what you want.

flash [flæʃ] n. 섬광
A flash is a sudden burst of light or of something shiny or bright.

reflect [riflékt] v. 비치다
To reflect means to show the image of someone or something on the surface of something such as a mirror, water or glass.

shatter [ʃǽtər] v. 산산조각 나다
If something shatters or is shattered, it breaks into a lot of small pieces.

pent-up [pènt-ʌ́p] a. 갇힌
Pent-up emotions, energies, or forces have been held back and not expressed, used, or released.

deluge [délju:dʒ] n. 폭우, 호우
A deluge is a sudden, very heavy fall of rain.

head [hed] v. (특정 방향으로) 향하게 하다
If you are headed for a particular place, you go toward that place.

take off idiom (특히 서둘러) 떠나다
To take off means to leave a place, especially in a hurry.

17 & 18

1. What was Ember trying to save?

    A. The Blue Flame

    B. Bernie and Cinder

    C. The shop's sign

    D. Her scooter

2. What surrounded Ember and Wade in the hearth?

    A. A rainbow

    B. Fire

    C. Steam

    D. Butterflies

3. **Why did Ember hand the lantern with the Blue Flame to her father?**

   A. To declare she wanted to run the shop

   B. To tell her father that she did not want to run the shop

   C. To tell her father that it was her dream to run the shop

   D. To bring wade back

4. **What did Ember do as a sign of respect to Bernie?**

   A. She cried for him.

   B. She gave him a gift.

   C. She gave him the Big Bow.

   D. She made him a glass cylinder.

5. **Why was Ember leaving her parents?**

   A. To go on a trip

   B. To open a new shop

   C. To apply for a job

   D. To work at a company

Check Your Reading Speed

1분에 몇 단어를 읽는지 리딩 속도를 측정해 보세요.

$$\frac{1{,}267 \text{ words}}{\text{reading time ( ) sec}} \times 60 = (\quad) \text{ WPM}$$

Build Your Vocabulary

one-way [wʌn-wéi] a. 편도의
In one-way streets or traffic systems, vehicles can only travel along in one direction.

gather [gǽðər] v. 모이다
If people gather somewhere or if someone gathers people somewhere, they come together in a group.

blubber [blʌbər] v. 흐느껴 울다
If someone blubbers, they cry noisily and in an unattractive way.

well [wel] v. (액체가) 솟아 나오다
If liquids, for example tears, well, they come to the surface and form a pool.

awash [əwáʃ] a. ~으로 넘치는
If someone is awash in something, they have a lot of it, often too much.

depict [dipíkt] v. 그리다
To depict someone or something means to show or represent them in a work of art such as a drawing or painting.

burst [bəːrst] v. (burst-burst) 갑자기 ~하다
If you burst into tears, laughter, or song, you suddenly begin to cry, laugh, or sing.

spot [spat] v. 발견하다
If you spot something or someone, you notice them.

flicker [flíkər] v. (불·빛 등이) 깜박거리다
If a light or flame flickers, it shines unsteadily.

murmur [mə́ːrmə] v. 중얼거리다
If you murmur something, you say it very quietly so that not many people can hear what you are saying.

rush [rʌʃ] v. (물이) 세차게 흐르다
If air or liquid rushes somewhere, it flows there suddenly and quickly.

culvert [kʌ́lvərt] n. 지하 배수로
A culvert is a tunnel that carries water under a road.

slam [slæm] v. 부딪치다
If one thing slams into or against another, it crashes into it with great force.

elevated [éləvèitid] a. (주변이나 지면보다) 높은
If land or buildings are elevated, they are raised up higher than the surrounding area.

crash [kræʃ] v. 부딪치다, 박살나다
If something crashes somewhere, it moves and hits something else violently, making a loud noise.

pull off idiom 벗어나다
If a vehicle or driver pulls off the road, the vehicle stops by the side of the road.

race [reis] v. ~을 앞지르려고 질주하다
If you race someone or something, you move very fast to compete against them.

raging [réidʒiŋ] a. 걷잡을 수 없이 거센
Raging water moves very forcefully and violently.

rev [rev] v. (엔진의) 회전 속도를 올리다
When you rev a vehicle, the engine speed is increased.

soar [sɔːr] v. 날아오르다
If something such as a bird soars into the air, it goes quickly up into the air.

holler [hálər] v. 소리지르다, 고함치다
If you holler, you shout loudly.

watch out idiom 조심해!
You say 'watch out,' when you warn someone about something dangerous.

panic [pǽnik] v. 어쩔 줄 모르다
If you panic or if someone panics you, you suddenly feel anxious or afraid, and act quickly and without thinking carefully.

safety [séifti] n. 안전한 곳
If you reach safety, you reach a place where you are safe from danger.

urge [əːrdʒ] v. 재촉하다
If you urge someone somewhere, you make them go there by touching them or talking to them.

near [niər] v. 가까이 가다
When you near a place, you come closer to it.

grand [grænd] a. 화려한
If you describe an activity or experience as grand, you mean that it is very pleasant and enjoyable.

reopening [ríóupəniŋ] n. 재개장
A reopening is the act of opening again something that was closed.

instantly [ínstəntli] ad. 즉시
If something happens instantly, it happens at once.

grab [græb] v. 움켜잡다
If you grab something, you take it or pick it up suddenly and roughly.

tug [tʌg] v. 잡아당기다
If you tug something, you pull it suddenly and strongly.

hydroplane [háidrouplein] v. 미끄러짐 현상을 일으키다
If something hydroplanes, it slides out of control on a wet road.

splash [splæʃ] v. 튀기다, 끼얹다
If a liquid splashes, it hits someone or something and scatters in a lot of small drops.

streak [striːk] n. 줄기, 가닥
If you have a streak of pain, the pain hurts you as it is moving in a long thin line.

leap [liːp] v. 뛰어오르다; n. 뜀, 도약
If you leap somewhere, you move there suddenly and quickly.

cab [kæb] n. 운전석
The cab of a truck or train is the front part in which the driver sits.

lunge [lʌndʒ] v. 달려들다
If you lunge in a particular direction, you move in that direction suddenly and clumsily.

yell [jel] v. 소리치다
If you yell, you shout loudly, usually because you are excited, angry, or in pain.

float [flout] v. (물 위나 공중에서) 떠다니다, 흘러가다
If something or someone is floating in a liquid, they are in the liquid, on or just below the surface, and are being supported by it.

debris [dəbríː] n. 파편
Debris is pieces from something that has been destroyed or pieces of rubbish or unwanted material that are spread around.

risk [risk] v. 위태롭게 하다, 걸다
If you risk your life or something else important, you behave in a way that might result in it being lost or harmed.

gush [gʌʃ] v. 솟구치다
When liquid gushes out of something, or when something gushes a liquid, the liquid flows out very quickly and in large quantities.

gasp [gæsp] v. 헉 하고 숨을 쉬다
When you gasp, you take a short quick breath through your mouth, especially when you are surprised or shocked.

spout [spaut] n. (액체의) 분출
A spout of liquid is a long stream of it which is coming out of something very forcefully.

jet [dʒet] v. 분출하다
If a liquid or gas jets out from somewhere, it comes quickly out of a small hole.

weight [weit] n. 무게, 체중
If you move your weight, you change position so that most of the pressure of your body is on a particular part of your body.

nip [nip] v. 물다, 꼬집다
If something nips you, it gives you a small, sharp bite.

muffled [mʌfld] a. 소리를 죽인
Muffled sounds cannot be heard clearly.

grunt [grʌnt] n. 끙 하는 소리
A grunt is a short, low sound made by a person or an animal.

materialize [mətíəriəlàiz] v. (갑자기) 나타나다
If a person or thing materializes, they suddenly appear, after they have been invisible or in another place.

smush [smʌʃ] v. 으깨다
If something is smushed, it is smashed or crushed.

gesture [dʒésʧər] v. 가리키다, 몸짓을 하다
If you gesture, you use movements of your hands or head in order to tell someone something or draw their attention to something.

keyhole [kíːhòul] n. (자물쇠의) 열쇠 구멍
A keyhole is the hole in a lock that you put a key in.

lock [lak] n. 잠금장치
The lock on something such as a door or a drawer is the device which is used to keep it shut and prevent other people from opening it.

squeeze [skwiːz] v. 비집고 들어가다
If you squeeze a person or thing somewhere or if they squeeze there, they manage to get through or into a small space.

reform [rifɔ́ːrm] v. 형태를 다시 잡다
To reform means to change the shape of or to make changes to something.

heroic [hiróuik] a. 영웅적인
If you describe a person or their actions as heroic, you admire them because they show extreme bravery.

entrance [éntrəns] n. 등장; 입구
You can refer to someone's arrival in a place as their entrance, especially when you think that they are trying to be noticed and admired.

spring into action idiom 갑자기 행동하기 시작하다
If things or people spring into action or spring to life, they suddenly start being active or suddenly come into existence.

side by side idiom 나란히
If two people or things are side by side, they are next to each other.

hold back idiom 저지하다
If you hold back someone or something, you prevent them from moving forward or crossing something.

counter [káuntər] n. 계산대
In a place such as a shop or café, a counter is a long narrow table or flat surface at which customers are served.

shelf [ʃelf] n. (pl. shelves) 선반
A shelf is a flat piece of wood, plastic, or glass that is attached to the wall or is part of a piece of furniture, used for putting things on.

pile [pail] v. 쌓다, 포개다
If you pile things somewhere, you put them there so that they form a pile.

cauldron [kɔ́:ldrən] n. 솥, 큰 냄비
A cauldron is a very large, round metal pot used for cooking over a fire.

flare [flɛər] v. 확 타오르다
When a fire flares up, it suddenly burns more intensely.

melt [melt] v. 녹이다
When a solid substance melts or when you melt it, it changes to a liquid, usually because it has been heated.

cling [kliŋ] v. (clung-clung) 매달리다
If you cling to something, you hold on it tightly.

violent [váiələnt] a. 격렬한
If you describe something as violent, you mean that it is said, done, or felt very strongly.

churn [ʧə́:rn] v. 마구 휘돌다
If water, mud, or dust churns, it moves about violently.

smash [smæʃ] v. 부수다
If you smash something, it breaks into many pieces, for example when it is hit or dropped.

tumble [tʌmbl] v. 굴러 떨어지다
If someone or something tumbles somewhere, they fall there with a rolling or bouncing movement.

cylinder [sílindər] n. 원통형 용기
A cylinder is an object with flat circular ends and long straight sides.

plead [pli:d] v. 애원하다
If you plead with someone to do something, you ask them in an intense, emotional way to do it.

struggle [strʌgl] v. 노력하다, 애쓰다
If you struggle to do something, you try hard to do it, even though other people or things may be making it difficult for you to succeed.

in place idiom 제자리에
If something is in place, it is in the correct position.

sweep [swi:p] v. (swept-swept) (거칠게) 휩쓸고 가다
If wind, a stormy sea, or another strong force sweeps someone or something along, it moves them quickly along.

roar [rɔ:r] v. 웅웅거리다
If something roars, it makes a very loud noise.

brick [brik] n. 벽돌
Bricks are rectangular blocks of baked clay used for building walls, which are usually red or brown.

topple [tapl] v. 넘어지다
If someone or something topples somewhere or if you topple them, they become unsteady or unstable and fall over.

expose [ikspóuz] v. 드러내다
To expose something that is usually hidden means to uncover it so that it can be seen.

hearth [ha:rθ] n. 난로
The hearth is the floor of a fireplace, and the area in front of it.

seal [si:l] v. 밀폐하다, 틈을 막다
If you seal something in a container, you put it inside and then close the container tightly.

grip [grip] v. 꽉 잡다
If you grip something, you take hold of it with your hand and continue to hold it firmly.

glance [glæns] v. 흘깃 보다
If you glance at something or someone, you look at them very quickly and then look away again immediately.

extinguish [ikstíŋgwiʃ] v. (불을) 끄다
If you extinguish a fire or a light, you stop it burning or shining.

pop [pap] v. 불쑥 나타나다
If someone or something pops, it appears suddenly or unexpectedly.

flinch [flinʧ] v. 움찔하다
If you flinch, you make a small sudden movement, especially when something surprises you or hurts you.

seep [si:p] v. 스며들다
If something such as liquid or gas seeps somewhere, it flows slowly and in small amounts into a place where it should not go.

trickle [tríkl] v. (액체가) 흐르다
When a liquid trickles, it flows slowly in very small amounts.

leak [li:k] n. (액체·기체의) 누출
A leak means liquid or gas that escapes through a hole in something.

chimney stack [ʧímni stæk] n. (지붕 위로 나와 있는) 굴뚝
A chimney stack is the brick or stone part of a chimney that is above the roof of a building.

cascade [kæskéid] v. 폭포처럼 흐르다
If water cascades somewhere, it pours or flows downward very fast and in large quantities.

collapse [kəlǽps] v. 붕괴되다
If a building or other structure collapses, it falls down very suddenly.

evaporate [ivǽpərèit] v. 증발하다
When a liquid evaporates, it changes from a liquid state to a gas, because its temperature has increased.

alarming [əlá:rmiŋ] a. 놀라운, 심상치 않은
Something that is alarming makes you feel afraid or anxious that something unpleasant or dangerous might happen.

rate [reit] n. 속도
The rate at which something happens is the speed with which it happens.

snuff [snʌf] v. (불을) 끄다
If you snuff out a small flame, you stop it burning, usually by using your fingers or by covering it with something for a few seconds.

full-on [ful-ɔ́n] a. 최대의, 극도의
Full-on is used to describe things or activities that have all the characteristics of their type, or are done in the strongest or most extreme way possible.

regret [rigrét] n. 후회
Regret is a feeling of sadness or disappointment, which is caused by something that has happened or something that you have done or not done.

surround [səráund] v. 둘러싸다
If a person or thing is surrounded by something, that thing is located all around them.

sorrow [sárou] n. 슬픔, 비통
Sorrow is a feeling of deep sadness or regret.

vulnerable [vʌ́lnərəbl] a. 약한
Something that is vulnerable can be easily harmed or affected by something bad.

cast [kæst] v. (cast-cast) (그림자를) 드리우다
If something casts a light or shadow somewhere, it causes it to appear there.

whisper [hwíspər] v. 속삭이다
When you whisper, you say something very quietly, using your breath rather than your throat, so that only one person can hear you.

embrace [imbréis] v. 포옹하다
If you embrace someone, you put your arms around them and hold them tightly, usually in order to show your love or affection for them.

silence [sáiləns] n. 침묵
If there is silence, nobody is speaking.

Check Your Reading Speed

1분에 몇 단어를 읽는지 리딩 속도를 측정해 보세요.

$$\frac{1{,}196 \text{ words}}{\text{reading time (} \quad \text{) sec}} \times 60 = (\qquad) \text{ WPM}$$

Build Your Vocabulary

recede [risíːd] v. 물러나다, 멀어지다
If something recedes from you, it moves away.

damp [dæmp] a. 축축한
Something that is damp is slightly wet.

debris [dəbríː] n. 파편
Debris is pieces from something that has been destroyed or pieces of rubbish or unwanted material that are spread around.

desperate [déspərət] a. 간절히 원하는
If you are desperate to do something, you want or need it very much indeed.

hearth [haːrθ] n. 난로
The hearth is the floor of a fireplace, and the area in front of it.

element [éləmənt] n. 원소
An element is one of the four substances (earth, air, fire, and water) from which people used to believe that everything was made.

knock [nak] v. (움직이도록) 치다
If you knock something, you touch or hit it roughly, especially so that it falls or moves.

opening [óupəniŋ] n. 구멍, 통로
An opening is a hole or empty space through which things or people can pass.

kneel [niːl] v. (knelt-knelt) 무릎을 꿇다
When you kneel, you bend your legs so that your knees are touching the ground.

brick [brik] n. 벽돌
Bricks are rectangular blocks of baked clay used for building walls, which are usually red or brown.

illuminate [ilú:mənèit] v. 비추다
To illuminate something means to shine light on it and to make it brighter and more visible.

flicker [flíkər] n. (빛의) 깜박거림
A flicker of something is a light that shines in an unsteady way.

flame [fleim] n. 불꽃
A flame is the hot, bright, and burning gas produced by something on fire.

dim [dim] a. 흐릿한
Dim light is not bright.

soothe [su:ð] v. 달래다
If you soothe someone who is angry or upset, you make them feel calmer.

embrace [imbréis] n. 포옹; v. 포옹하다
An embrace is an act of putting your arms around someone as a sign of love.

shaky [ʃéiki] a. 떨리는
If your body or your voice is shaky, you cannot control it properly and it shakes, for example because you are ill or nervous.

take a breath idiom 심호흡을 하다
If you say that you took a breath before doing something dangerous or frightening, you mean that you tried to make yourself feel strong and confident.

admit [ædmít] v. 인정하다
If you admit something, you agree, often unwillingly, that it is true.

realize [rí:əlàiz] v. 인식하다, 자각하다
If you realize something, you become aware of it, understand it, or accept it after thinking about it or discovering it.

thick [θik] a. (목소리가) 잠긴
If someone's voice is thick, they are not speaking clearly, for example because they are ill or upset.

sob [sab] v. 흐느끼며 말하다
If you sob something, you say it while you are crying.

whimper [hwímpər] n. (사람이) 훌쩍거림; v. 훌쩍이다
A whimper is a low, weak sound that a person or an animal makes when they are hurt, frightened or sad.

chimney [ʧímni] n. 굴뚝
A chimney is a pipe through which smoke goes up into the air, usually through the roof of a building.

bucket [bʌ́kit] n. 양동이, 들통
A bucket is a round metal or plastic container with a handle attached to its sides.

glance [glæns] v. 흘낏 보다
If you glance at something or someone, you look at them very quickly and then look away again immediately.

stare [stɛər] v. 빤히 쳐다보다
If you stare at someone or something, you look at them for a long time.

windshield [wíndʃiːld] n. (자동차 등의) 앞유리
The windshield of a car or other vehicle is the glass window at the front through which the driver looks.

plunk [plʌŋk] v. 쿵 하고 떨어지다
If something plunks, it hits and produces a quick, hollow, metallic, or harsh sound.

surge [səːrdʒ] n. (강한 감정이) 치밀어 오름
If you feel a surge of a particular emotion or feeling, you experience it suddenly and powerfully.

deathbed [déθbèd] n. 임종(의 자리)
If someone is on their deathbed, they are in a bed and about to die.

league [liːg] n. 수준
You use the word league to make comparisons between different people or things, especially in terms of their quality.

scared [skɛərd] a. 무서워하는, 겁먹은
If you are scared of someone or something, you are frightened of them.

bawl [bɔ́ːl] v. (시끄럽게) 울어대다
If you say that a child is bawling, you are annoyed because it is crying loudly.

realization [rìːəlizéiʃən] n. 깨달음
Realization means the process of becoming aware of something.

dawn [dɔːn] v. 점점 분명해지다
If something dawns in, it becomes obvious.

gaze [geiz] v. 응시하다, 바라보다
To gaze at something or someone means to look steadily and intently, especially in admiration, surprise, or thought.

match [mæʧ] n. 어울리는 사람
If a combination of things or people is a good match, they have a pleasing effect when placed or used together.

announce [ənáuns] v. 큰 소리로 알리다
To announce means to say something in a loud and often serious way.

pour [pɔːr] v. 마구 쏟아지다
When a liquid or other substance pours somewhere, for example through a hole, it flows quickly and in large quantities.

scratch [skræʧ] v. (가려운 데를) 긁다
If you scratch yourself, you rub your fingernails against your skin because it is itching.

ban [bæn] v. 금지하다
To ban something means to state officially that it must not be done, shown, or used.

wail [weil] v. 울부짖다, 통곡하다
If someone wails, they make a long, loud, high-pitched sound because they are sad or in pain.

puddle [pʌdl] n. 웅덩이
A puddle is a small pool of liquid, especially water, that has collected on the ground.

explore [iksplɔ́ːr] v. 탐험하다
If you explore a place, you go around it where you have never been in order to find out what is there.

droplet [dráplit] n. 작은 (물)방울
A droplet is a very small drop of liquid.

peer [piər] v. 유심히 보다
If you peer at something, you look at it very hard, usually because it is difficult to see clearly.

locate [lóukeit] v. 정확한 위치를 찾아내다
If you locate something or someone, you find out where they are.

glow [glou] v. 빛나다
When something glows, it produces a steady light.

breathtaking [bréθteikiŋ] a. (너무 아름답거나 놀라워서) 숨이 막히는
If you say that something is breathtaking, you are emphasizing that it is extremely beautiful or amazing.

light up idiom 환하게 만들다
If you light something up, it becomes bright, usually when you shine light on it.

declare [dikléər] v. 분명히 말하다
If you declare that something is true, you say that it is true in a firm, deliberate way.

beam [biːm] v. 환하게 웃다
If you beam, you smile very happily.

chuckle [ʧʌkl] v. 빙그레 웃다
When you chuckle, you laugh quietly.

recover [rikʌ́vər] v. 회복하다
If something recovers from a period of weakness or difficulty, it improves or gets stronger again.

restore [ristɔ́ːr] v. 복구하다
To restore someone or something to a previous condition means to cause them to be in that condition once again.

bustle [bʌsl] v. 붐비다, 북적거리다
A place that is bustling with people or activity is full of people who are very busy or lively.

log [lɔːg] n. 통나무
A log is a piece of a thick branch or of the trunk of a tree that has been cut so that it can be used for fuel or for making things.

lava [láːvə] n. 용암
Lava is the very hot liquid rock that comes out of a volcano.

steam [stiːm] v. 증기를 내뿜다
If something steams, it gives off the gas that water produces when it is boiled.

crunch [krʌnʧ] v. 아작아작 씹다
If you crunch something hard, such as a sweet, you crush it noisily between your teeth.

crackly [krǽkli] a. 탁탁 소리를 내는
Something that is crackly makes a lot of short, harsh noises.

apron [éiprən] n. 앞치마
An apron is a piece of clothing that you put on over the front of your normal clothes and tie round your waist.

ladder [lǽdər] n. 사다리
A ladder is a piece of equipment for reaching high places that consists of two bars and smaller pieces to be used as steps.

reveal [riví:l] v. 드러내 보이다
To reveal something means to make people aware of it.

armpit [á:rmpìt] n. 겨드랑이
Your armpits are the areas of your body under your arms where your arms join your shoulders.

yank [jæŋk] v. 홱 잡아당기다
If you yank someone or something somewhere, you pull them there suddenly and with a lot of force.

yelp [jelp] v. 비명을 지르다
If a person or dog yelps, they give a sudden short cry, often because of fear or pain.

giggle [gigl] v. 피식 웃다, 킥킥거리다
If someone giggles, they laugh in a childlike way, because they are amused, nervous, or embarrassed.

browse [brauz] v. 둘러보다
If you browse in a shop, you look at things in a fairly casual way, in the hope that you might find something you like.

merchandise [mə́:rʧəndàiz] n. 상품
Merchandise is goods that are bought, sold, or traded.

shut down idiom (공장·가게의) 문을 닫다
If a factory or business shuts down or if someone shuts it down, work there stops or it no longer trades as a business.

stock [stak] v. 채우다
To stock something such as a shelf or a shop means to fill it with goods or supplies.

shelf [ʃelf] n. (pl. shelves) 선반
A shelf is a flat piece of wood, plastic, or glass that is attached to the wall or is part of a piece of furniture, used for putting things on.

accidentally [æksədéntəli] ad. 우연히, 뜻하지 않게
If something occurs accidentally, it happens in an accidental or unintended manner.

earth [əːrθ] n. 흙
Earth is the substance in which plants grow that covers most of the land.

apologize [əpálədʒàiz] v. 사과하다
To apologize means to express regret for something wrong that one has done.

pump [pʌmp] v. 흔들다, 움직이다
To pump means to move something very quickly in and out or up and down.

fist [fist] n. 주먹
Your hand is referred to as your fist when you have bent your fingers in toward the palm in order to hit someone, to make an angry gesture, or to hold something.

instantly [ínstəntli] ad. 즉시
If something happens instantly, it happens at once.

smitten [smítn] a. ~에게 반한
If you are smitten, you find someone so attractive that you are or seem to be in love with them.

counter [káuntər] n. 계산대
In a place such as a shop or café, a counter is a long narrow table or flat surface at which customers are served.

retirement [ritáiərmənt] n. 은퇴
A person's retirement is the period in their life after they have stopped work, usually because you have reach a particular age.

burst [bəːrst] v. (burst-burst) 갑자기 ~하다
If you burst into tears, laughter, or song, you suddenly begin to cry, laugh, or sing.

greet [griːt] v. 인사하다, 맞이하다
To greet someone means to say hello to them or to welcome them.

include [inklúːd] v. 포함하다
If one thing includes another thing, it has the other thing as one of its parts.

good-naturedly [gud-néitʃərdli] ad. 친절히
If you do something good-naturedly, you do it in a kind or friendly manner, especially when dealing with people.

dock [dak] n. 부두
A dock is an enclosed area in a harbor where ships go to be loaded, unloaded, and repaired.

grand [grænd] a. 웅장한
If you describe a building or a piece of scenery as grand, you mean that its size or appearance is very impressive.

board [bɔːrd] v. 탑승하다
When you board a train, ship, or aircraft, you get on it in order to travel somewhere.

passenger [pǽsəndʒər] n. 승객
A passenger in a vehicle such as a bus, boat, or plane is a person who is traveling in it, but who is not driving it or working on it.

blubber [blʌ́bər] v. 흐느껴 울다
If someone blubbers, they cry noisily and in an unattractive way.

drip [drip] n. (액체가) 뚝뚝 떨어지는 소리
Drip means the sound or action of small drops of liquid falling continuously.

shoot [ʃuːt] v. (shot-shot) (눈길 등을) 휙 던지다
If you shoot a look at someone, you look at them quickly and briefly, often in a way that expresses your feelings.

grin [grin] v. 활짝 웃다
When you grin, you smile broadly.

expression [ikspréʃən] n. 표정
Your expression is the way that your face looks at a particular moment.

end up idiom 결국 ~하게 되다
If you end up doing something or end up in a particular place or situation, you find yourself doing it or in that place or situation that you did not expect or intend to be in.

scold [skould] v. 야단치다
If you scold someone, you speak angrily to them because they have done something wrong.

nudge [nʌdʒ] n. (팔꿈치로 살짝) 쿡 찌르기
A nudge is a slight push, usually with the elbow.

luggage [lʌ́gidʒ] n. 짐, 수하물
Luggage refers to the bags and suitcases that contain a traveler's personal belongings.

stretch [streʧ] v. (팔·다리를) 뻗다
If you stretch your arms or legs out, you move them away from your body to reach something.

bow [bau] n. (고개 숙여 하는) 인사, 절
A bow is the act of bending your head or the upper part of your body forward in order to say hello or goodbye to someone or to show respect.

gasp [gæsp] v. 헉 하고 숨을 쉬다
When you gasp, you take a short quick breath through your mouth, especially when you are surprised or shocked.

respectful [rispéktfəl] a. 경의를 표하는
If you are respectful, you show respect for someone.

gesture [dʒésʧər] n. 몸짓
A gesture is a movement that you make with a part of your body.

tremendous [triméndəs] a. 엄청난
You use tremendous to emphasize how strong a feeling or quality is, or how large an amount is.

weight [weit] n. (무거운 책임감 같은) 짐, 부담
The weight of something is a great responsibility or worry.

horn [hɔːrn] n. 경적
On a vehicle such as a car, the horn is the device that makes a loud noise as a signal or warning.

summon [sʌmən] v. (용기 등을 어렵게) 내다
If you summon up the courage or strength, you make a great effort to do something.

courage [kɔ́ːridʒ] n. 용기
Courage is the quality shown by someone who decides to do something difficult or dangerous, even though they may be afraid.

security [sikjúərəti] n. 안도감, 안심
A feeling of security is a feeling of being safe and free from worry.

수고하셨습니다!

드디어 끝까지 다 읽으셨군요! 축하드립니다! 여러분은 이 책을 통해 총 23,756개의 단어를 읽으셨고, 1,000개 이상의 어휘와 표현들을 공부하셨습니다. 이 책에 나온 어휘는 다른 원서를 읽을 때도 빈번히 만날 수 있는 필수 어휘들입니다. 이 책을 읽었던 경험은 비슷한 수준의 다른 원서들을 읽을 때 큰 도움이 될 것입니다. 이제 자신의 상황에 맞게 원서를 반복해서 읽거나, 오디오북을 들어 볼 수 있습니다. 혹은 비슷한 수준의 다른 원서를 찾아 읽는 것도 좋습니다. 일단 원서를 완독한 뒤에 어떻게 계속 영어 공부를 이어갈 수 있을지, 아래에 제시되는 도움말을 꼼꼼히 살펴 보고 각자 상황에 맞게 적용해 보세요!

리딩(Reading)을 확실하게 다지고 싶다면? 반복해서 읽어 보세요!

리딩 실력을 탄탄하게 다지고 싶다면, 같은 원서를 2~3번 반복해서 읽을 것을 권합니다. 같은 책을 여러 번 읽으면 지루할 것 같지만, 꼭 그렇지도 않습니다. 반복해서 읽을 때 처음과 주안점을 다르게 두면, 전혀 다른 느낌으로 재미있게 읽을 수 있습니다.

처음 원서를 읽을 때는 생소한 단어들과 스토리로 인해 읽으면서 곧바로 이해하기가 매우 힘들 수 있습니다. 전체 맥락을 잡고 읽어도 약간 버거운 느낌이지요. 하지만 반복해서 읽기 시작하면 달라집니다. 일단 내용을 파악한 상황이기 때문에 문장 구조나 어휘의 활용에 더 집중하게 되고, 조금 더 깊이 있게 읽을 수 있게 됩니다. 좋은 표현과 문장을 수집하고 메모할 만한 여유도 생기게 되지요. 어휘도 많이 익숙해졌기 때문에 리딩 속도에도 탄력이 붙습니다. 처음 읽을 때는 '내용'에서 재미를 느꼈다면, 반복해서 읽을 때는 '영어'에서 재미를 느끼게 되는 것입니다. 따라서 리딩 실력을 더욱 확고하게 다지고자 한다면, 같은 책을 2~3회 정도 반복해서 읽을 것을 권해 드립니다.

리스닝(Listening) 실력을 늘리고 싶다면? 귀를 통해서 읽어 보세요!

많은 영어 학습자들이 '리스닝이 안 돼서 문제'라고 한탄합니다. 그리고 리스닝 실력을 늘리는 방법으로 무슨 뜻인지 몰라도 반복해서 듣는 '무작정 듣기'를 선택합니다. 하지만 뜻도 모르면서 무작정 듣는 것은 엄청난 인내력이 필요합니다. 그래서 대부분 며칠 시도하다가 포기해 버리고 말지요.

따라서 모르는 내용을 무작정 듣는 것보다는 어느 정도 알고 있는 내용을 반복해서 듣는 것이 더 효과적인 듣기 방법입니다. 그리고 이런 방식의 듣기에 활용할 수 있는 가장 좋은 교재가 오디오북입니다.

리스닝 실력을 향상하고 싶다면, 이 책에서 제공하는 오디오북을 이용해서 듣는 연습을 해 보세요. 활용법은 간단합니다. 일단 책을 한 번 완독했다면, 오디오북을 통해 다시 들어 보는 것입니다. 휴대 기기에 넣어 시간이 날 때 틈틈이 듣는 것도 좋고, 책상에 앉아 눈으로는 텍스트를 보며 귀로 읽는 것도 좋습니다. 이미 읽었던 내용이라 이해하기가 훨씬 수월하고, 애매했던 발음들도 자연스럽게 교정할 수 있습니다. 또 성우의 목소리 연기를 듣다 보면 내용이 더욱 생동감 있게 다가와 이해도가 높아지는 효과도 거둘 수 있습니다.

반대로 듣기에 자신이 있는 사람이라면, 책을 읽기 전에 처음부터 오디오북을 먼저 듣는 것도 좋은 방법입니다. 귀를 통해 책을 쭉 읽어 보고, 이후에 다시 눈으로 책을 읽으면서 잘 들리지 않았던 부분을 보충하는 것이지요.

중요한 것은 내용을 따라가면서, 내용에 푹 빠져서 반복해 들어야 한다는 것입니다. 이렇게 연습을 반복해서 눈으로 읽지 않은 책이라도 '귀를 통해' 읽을 수 있을 정도가 되면, 리스닝으로 고생하는 일은 거의 없을 것입니다.

왼쪽의 QR코드를 스마트폰으로 인식하면 오디오북 MP3와 한국어 번역 파일을 다운로드할 수 있는 링크로 연결됩니다. 더불어 롱테일북스 홈페이지(www.longtailbooks.co.kr)에서도 오디오북과 한국어 번역 파일을 다운로드 받을 수 있습니다.

스피킹(Speaking)이 고민이라면? 소리 내어 읽어 보세요!

스피킹 역시 많은 학습자들이 고민하는 부분입니다. 스피킹이 고민이라면, 원서를 큰 소리로 읽는 낭독 훈련(Voice Reading)을 해 보세요!

'소리 내어 읽는 것이 말하기에 정말로 도움이 될까?'라고 의아한 생각이 들 수도 있습니다. 하지만 인간의 두뇌 입장에서 봤을 때, 성대 구조를 활용해서 '발화'한다는 점에서는 소리 내어 읽기와 말하기는 큰 차이가 없다고 합니다. 소리 내어 읽는 것은 '타인의 생각'을 전달하고, 직접 말하는 것은 '자신의 생각'을 전달한다는 차이가 있을 뿐, 머릿속에서 문장을 처리하고 조음 기관(혀와 성대 등)을 움직여 의미를 만든다는 점에서 같은 과정인 것이지요. 따라서 소리 내서 읽는 연습을 꾸준히 하는 것은 스피킹 연습에 큰 도움이 됩니다.

소리 내어 읽기를 하는 방법도 간단합니다. 일단 오디오북을 들으면서 성우의 목소리를 최대한 따라 하며 같이 읽어 보세요. 발음뿐 아니라, 억양, 어조, 느낌까지 완벽히 따라 한다고 생각하면서 소리 내어 읽습니다. 따라 읽는 것이 조금 익숙해지면, 옆의 누군가에게 이 책을 읽어 준다는 생각으로 소리 내어 계속 읽어 나갑니다. 한 번 눈과 귀로 읽었던 책이기 때문에 보다 수월하게 진행할 수 있고, 자연스럽게 어휘와 표현을 복습하는 효과도 거두게 됩니다. 또 이렇게 소리 내어 읽은 것을 녹음해서 들어 보면 스스로에게 좋은 피드백이 됩니다.

라이팅(Writing)까지 욕심이 난다면? 요약하는 연습을 해 보세요!

원서를 라이팅 연습에 직접적으로 활용하는 데에는 한계가 있지만, 적절히 활용하면 원서도 유용한 라이팅 자료가 될 수 있습니다.

특히 책을 읽고 그 내용을 요약하는 연습은 큰 도움이 됩니다. 요약 훈련의 방식도 간단합니다. 원서를 읽고 그날 읽은 분량만큼 혹은 책을 다 읽고 전체 내용을 기반으로, 책 내용을 한번 요약하고 나의 느낌을 영어로 적어 보는 것입니다.

이때 그 책에 나왔던 단어와 표현을 최대한 활용해서 요약하는 것이 중요합니다. 영어 표현력은 결국 얼마나 다양한 어휘로 많은 표현을 해 보았느냐가 좌우하게 됩니다. 이런 면에서 내가 읽은 책을, 그 책에 나온 문장과 어휘로 다시 표현해 보는 것은 매우 효율적인 방법입니다. 책에 나온 어휘와 표현을 단순히 읽고 무슨 말인지 아는 정도가 아니라, 실제로 직접 활용해서 쓸 수 있을 만큼 확실하게 익히게 되는 것이지요. 여기에 첨삭까지 받을 수 있는 방법이 있다면 금상첨화입니다. 이러한 '표현하기' 연습은 스피킹 훈련에도 그대로 적용될 수 있습니다. 책을 읽고 그 내용을 3분 안에 다른 사람에게 영어로 말하는 연습을 해 보세요. 순발력과 표현력을 기르는 좋은 훈련이 될 것입니다.

'스피드 리딩 카페'에서 함께 원서를 읽어 보세요!

원서 읽기를 활용한 영어 공부에 관심이 있으시다면, 국내 최대 영어원서 읽기 동호회 스피드 리딩 카페(http://cafe.naver.com/readingtc)를 방문해 보세요. 이미 수만 명의 회원들이 모여서 '북클럽'을 통해 함께 원서를 읽고 있습니다. 13만 명이 넘는 회원들이 단순히 함께 원서를 읽는 것뿐만 아니라, 위에서 언급한 다양한 방식으로 원서를 활용하여 영어 실력을 실질적으로 향상시키고 있습니다. 여러분도 스피드 리딩 카페를 방문해 보신다면 많은 자극과 도움을 받으실 수 있을 것입니다.

원서 읽기 습관을 길러 보세요!

일상에서 영어를 한마디도 쓰지 않는 비영어권 국가에서 살고 있는 우리가 영어 환경에 가장 쉽고, 편하고, 부담 없이 노출되는 방법은 바로 '영어원서 읽기'입니다. 언제 어디서든 원서를 붙잡고 읽기만 하면 곧바로 영어를 접하는 환경이 만들어지기 때문이지요. 하루에 20분씩만 꾸준히 읽는다면, 1년에 무려 120시간 동안 영어에 노출될 수 있습니다. 이런 이유 때문에 영어 교육 전문가들이 영어원서 읽기를 추천하는 것이지요.

영어원서를 꾸준히 읽어 보세요. '원서 읽기 습관'을 만들어 보세요! 이렇게 영어를 접하는 시간이 늘어나면, 영어 실력도 당연히 향상될 수밖에 없습니다.

아래 표에는 영어 수준별 추천 원서들이 있습니다. 하지만 이것은 절대적인 기준이 아니며, 학습자의 영어 수준과 관심 분야에 따라 개인적인 책 선정은 달라질 수 있습니다. 이 책은 Level 3에 해당합니다. 이 책의 완독 경험을 기준으로 삼아 적절한 책을 골라 꾸준히 읽어 보세요.

영어 수준별 추천 원서 목록

리딩 레벨	영어 수준	원서 목록
Level 1	유치원생 초등학생	「The Zack Files」 시리즈, 「Magic Tree House」 시리즈, 「Junie B. Jones」 시리즈, 「Horrid Henry」 시리즈, 로알드 달 단편들 (「The Giraffe and the Pelly and Me」, 「Esio Trot」, 「The Enormous Crocodile」, 「The Magic Finger」, 「Fantastic Mr. Fox」 등)
Level 2	초·중학생	「Spiderwick Chronicles」 시리즈, 쉬운 뉴베리 수상작들 (「Sarah, Plain and Tall」, 「The Hundred Dresses」 등), 앤드류 클레먼츠 단편들 (「Frindle」, 「The School Story」 등), 짧고 간단한 자기계발서 (「Who Moved My Cheese?」, 「The Present」 등)
Level 3	중·고등학생	「Wayside School」 시리즈, 「A Series of Unfortunate Events」 시리즈, 중간 수준의 뉴베리 수상작들 (「Number the Stars」 「Charlotte's Web」 등), 로알드 달 장편들 (「Charlie and the Chocolate Factory」, 「Matilda」 등)
Level 4	대학생	「Harry Potter」 시리즈 중 1~3권, 「Percy Jackson」 시리즈, 「The Chronicles of Narnia」 시리즈, 「The Alchemist」 어려운 수준의 뉴베리 수상작들 (「Holes」, 「The Giver」 등)
Level 5	이전 레벨의 원서 완독 유경험자	「Harry Potter」 시리즈 중 4~7권, 「Shopaholic」 시리즈, 「His Dark Materials」 시리즈, 「The Devil Wears Prada」, 「The Curious Incident of the Dog in the Night-Time」, 「Tuesdays With Morrie」 등

*참고 자료: Renaissance Learning, ReadingTown USA, Slyvan Learning Center

「영화로 읽는 영어원서」로 원서 읽기 습관을 만들어 보세요!

『엘리멘탈』을 재미있게 읽은 독자라면 「영화로 읽는 영어원서」 시리즈를 꾸준히 읽어 보시길 추천해 드립니다! 「영화로 읽는 영어원서」 시리즈는 유명 영화를 기반으로 한 소설판 영어원서로 보다 쉽고 부담 없이 원서 읽기를 시작할 수 있도록 도와주고, 오디오북을 기본적으로 포함해 원서의 활용 범위를 넓힌 책입니다.

『버즈 라이트이어』, 『엔칸토: 마법의 세계』, 『소울』, 『겨울왕국』, 『인사이드 아웃』, 『모아나』, 『주토피아』, 『코코』 등 출간하는 책마다 독자들의 큰 사랑을 받으며 어학 분야의 베스트셀러를 기록했고, 학원과 학교들에서도 꾸준히 교재로 채택되는 등 영어 학습자들에게도 좋은 반응을 얻고 있습니다. (전국 소재 중·고교 방과 후 보충 교재 채택, 전국 영어 학원 정·부교재 채택, 초등학교 영어원서 읽기 대회 교재 채택 등)

Prologue

1. C They traveled with only a few possessions from Fire Land, the home they'd left behind. A Blue Flame contained by a lantern was the most precious item of all. The Flame represented their Fire Land traditions and heritage.

2. B Inside the old structure, Bernie's mind raced, full of ideas for their new home. He would turn the first floor into a shop, a shrine to Fire Land where they would sell snacks and souvenirs inspired by their homeland.

3. A In the years that followed, Bernie and Cinder adjusted to living in Element City. While they learned a new language and new ways of doing things, Bernie also taught Ember the language, values, and customs of their homeland.

4. B He climbed down the ladder and stood beside Ember, admiring their work. "This shop is the dream of our family," he said. "And someday it will all be yours."

5. D Ember's eyes widened. From that moment on, this was what she would strive for, to be a good daughter and to take over the shop—her father's dream.

Chapters 1 & 2

1. D "Kol nuts coming up!" said Bernie. While her father rang up the order, Ember tapped the keys on her toy cash register. "Good daughter," Bernie said warmly.

2. B He and Ember squeezed logs in their palms to make bite-sized pieces of kol nuts and placed them on a plate. Ember handed the plate to the customer.

3. C "Just give me one for free!" demanded the customer. "That's not how this works!" Ember bellowed. Her flames flickered, turning purple, and then . . . KABOOM! She exploded."

4. A Many years later, Ember still recalled her father's words when she had a difficult customer—like right now. Take a breath, make a connection, she told herself.

5. B "Sorry, everyone," called Ember as her father hurried over. "Oh! Please forgive my daughter," Bernie added. "She burns bright, but sometimes too bright." He blew out a burning flower on the customer's hat. "Nice hat, by the way," he said. "Let me make you a new batch! On the house!"

Chapters 3 & 4

1. C As Clod plucked the flower, he let out an "Ow!" Then he knelt on the sidewalk and offered it to Ember in a grand gesture. "My queen." Ember took the flower. Poof! It burned to a crisp in her hand. "Sorry, buddy," she said. "Elements don't mix."

2. B "Come on!" Clod begged. "Go to the festival with me! You never leave this part of town." "That's because everything I need is right here," replied Ember. Just then, a Wetro train passed overhead, sending water splashing down. Ember glanced up, annoyed, as she popped open her umbrella. "Plus," she said, "this city wasn't made with Fire people in mind."

3. A Her smile faded when she saw how old Bernie looked. She was the reason he hadn't been able to retire. Because she wasn't ready. Because she still lost her temper.

4. C When she rolled up the shade on the window, a crowd of customers was waiting, but Ember kept her cool. She smiled and opened the door.

5. B The morning passed by in a blur. Amid the endless stream of customers and the constant ring of the cash register, Ember tried to stay calm. Her father was counting on her. But the customers had so many questions! . . . Ember was about to blow her top, too. It was all too much. She strained to keep her cool. But any moment now, she'd blow. She could almost feel her flames turning purple. "Back in five minutes!" Ember choked out through gritted teeth.

Chapters 5 & 6

1. B That was when the train burst out of the tunnel. As light flooded the train car, Ember saw that the other Fire Element was her own reflection flickering at the back of Wade's head!

2. B Inside the building, Wade placed his tickets in a canister. He loaded the canister into a vacuum tube and let it go. Foomp! Then he noticed flecks of colorful light dancing across the wall.

3. C The kids blocked Ember's path. Thinking fast, Ember popped open her umbrella and fired up her flames. Like a hot-air balloon, she floated high over the kids, gazing down at their amazed faces.

4. A Ember slowly walked home over the bridge, all the way back to the shop. When she got there, she saw the Closed sign hanging on the door. She gasped. "What? Already?" She burst into the shop. "Hello?" When Ember heard her father coughing in the basement, she rushed down the stairs. She couldn't believe what she was seeing. Pipes had burst and were leaking everywhere! Her parents were desperately trying to clean up the mess.

5. B After the storm, the restaurant was a pile of rubble. Most of the neighbors' buildings had been damaged, too. "But it was too painful to stay," said Cinder. "We needed to start over, somewhere new." And so they boarded a boat they had found on the beach. Bernie's parents watched as the boat pulled away from the shore. "It was the last time your father ever saw his family," said Cinder, her voice heavy. "That is why we came here. To build this. Our new life."

Chapters 7 & 8

1. C Ember couldn't help watching the exciting game. Then she remembered why they had come—to find Gale. "Where is she?" she asked, scanning the stadium. "Up there," Wade said, gesturing. "In that skybox." The Air woman in the skybox swelled like a purple storm cloud. "Come on!" she bellowed at the players and refs. Fear flickered in Ember's chest, but only for a moment. "Okay," she said, taking a deep breath. "Time to cancel some tickets."

2. B As the crowd booed, Lutz's spirit sank. "Lutz man," said Wade. "He's been in such a funk 'cause his mom has been sick." As if to prove Wade's point, an opponent stole the ball from Lutz. Boos rose from the agitated Windbreaker fans.

3. A Wade suddenly stood and shouted skyward. "We love you, Lutz!" He gestured for other fans to join the chant. "We love you, Lutz! We love you, Lutz! C'mon! We love you, Lutz! Everybody!" The crowd responded. Soon the chant rose from the stands. "We love you, Lutz! We love you, Lutz!"

4. D "Water? In Firetown?" said Gale. "Yeah?" said Ember, confused. "Water was shut off to there years ago," said Gale. "Forget the tickets. I'm gonna have to take apart your dad's shop to figure out what's going on!"

5. B "How did you even end up here?" Ember asked. Wade recalled the moment clearly. "Well, I was in the canals, checking the doors for leaks . . . when I found some water that

shouldn't have been there." He had dipped his finger in the puddle and tasted it. It was rusty, with a hint of motor oil. Suddenly, a rush of water had knocked Wade off his feet. Then he got sucked into a filtering system. Then, bam! He'd gotten jammed into a pipe that was clogged with debris.

Chapters 9 & 10

1. B From the rooftop of Bernie's shop, Ember and Wade looked out over the canals. But to get an even better view, Ember knew they needed to be higher. She slid a tarp off part of the chimney, which was topped with a smoke cap. When she melted the smoke cap off its stand, it toppled, nearly hitting Wade. He yelped and darted out of the way. Ember tied the tarp to the upside-down smoke cap. "You might want to step back," she warned. Then she threw the tarp high over her head and blew flames into it. The tarp inflated. Ember had made a makeshift hot-air balloon!

2. A Ember began to recall a childhood memory. "When I was a kid, my dad took me there because they had a Vivisteria tree. I'd always wanted to see one. It's the only flower that can thrive in any environment. Fire included." Ember remembered the sign advertising the blooming Vivisteria. She had grabbed her father's hand and run toward the station. But as they'd approached the entrance, a guard had stopped them. "I was so excited," Ember murmured. "But they said our fire was too dangerous and they wouldn't let us in."

3. C "Oh!" cried Flarry. "Your ceiling is dripping again." "More leaks?" Bernie grumbled, glancing up. "Don't worry," said Ember. She hopped onto a table and melted the leaky pipe shut with her hands. "This whole problem is going away. I can feel it."

4. B When the lights dimmed inside, Ember's flames shone bright. Too bright. All around her, audience members scowled. She pulled her hood tightly around her flames and slunk into her seat.

5. C Later, when Ember walked home alone under the elevated Wetro, it whizzed overhead, sending a wall of water down from the track. But this time, Ember didn't pop an umbrella. She longed to touch the water. She reached out her hand but hesitated a moment too long. The water vanished as the train disappeared along the tracks.

Chapters 11 & 12

1. B Wade popped his head out of a vase. "I got bad news," he said as he began pouring water from the other vases onto his head. With each pour, he grew taller and his body filled out.

2. C "Are you really a food inspector?" interrogated Bernie. "As far as you know, yeah," Wade said. "Then inspect this," said Bernie, gesturing toward the burning kol nuts. Ember stepped forward. "Dad . . . ," she began. Bernie silenced her. He pushed the bowl closer to Wade.

3. A That was when Wade noticed the sand beneath Ember. "Whoa, look what your fire did to the sand," he said. "It's glass!" Ember picked up a piece of glass and melted it in her hands. She formed it into a sphere and created a design inside, something that reflected how she was feeling.

4. B Suddenly, the earth began to vibrate. Ember gasped as an enormous boat passed through the canal, sending sheets of water into the culvert. Ember and Wade stared at the glass wall as the water rushed in behind it. They took a couple of steps backward, ready to run. But the glass held. Water splashed only into the bottom of the culvert behind the doors. "It worked!" cried Ember.

5. D The next night, Ember sat in her room, admiring the glass Vivisteria. She turned it over and over in her hands. Then she heard her father coughing. Ember hurried downstairs and found Bernie repairing a wall. When he coughed again, she asked, "Àshfá, you okay?" Bernie smiled. "Yes, yes. There's just too much to fix."

Chapters 13 & 14

1. C Ember picked up two large shards of glass and blew on them, melting them back together. "I can fix it," she reassured Alan. She gathered the rest of the broken pieces and melted them into a glowing liquid orb. Then she blew it into a shape resembling a pitcher.

2. B Wade realized he was going to need a different approach. He tried again. "Ember, when I met you, I thought I was drowning. But that light, that light inside you, has made me feel so alive. And all I want now is to be near it—near you. Together."

3. B For a few seconds, no one moved. Wade, Ember, and Wade's entire family were caught up in the moment. Then . . . Ring! Ring! The phone broke the silence.

4. A Ember smiled nervously as she turned to go. An internship at a glassmaking firm would be an amazing opportunity. But how could Ember ever leave her father and the shop? He needed her.

5. D Bernie smiled. "Well, since you are awake . . . I was going to tell you tomorrow, but I'm too excited to sleep. In two days, I retire!" "Oh!" said Ember. Cinder gasped. "Oh, Bernie!" "Two days?" asked Ember with a gulp. "Yes," said Bernie. "We are going to throw a big party. A grand reopening! That way I can tell the whole world my daughter is taking over."

Chapters 15 & 16

1. D Puzzled, Ember waved back. "Hey, Gale." She glanced at Wade. "What's going on?" "I know you think you have to end this," he began, "but that flooded tunnel? It goes to the main terminal." "Okay?" said Ember. "Do you still want to see a Vivisteria?" Wade asked.

2. B Gale blew even more air into the bubble, and Ember jumped in. Gale sealed it so no water could leak inside. Then Ember steadied herself and looked out at Wade, who gave her two thumbs up. It was working! Wade gently grabbed the bubble and started swimming down the flooded staircase. From the surface, Gale waved goodbye. With Ember in her protective bubble, Wade swam through the dark tunnel. Surrounded by water, Ember started to panic a little. But she remembered that Wade was by her side and she felt calmer.

3. A They stepped closer and pressed their palms together again, more firmly this time. Wade's water pushed back to match the strength of Ember's heat. Their hands tingled as they interlocked fingers. They had reached an equilibrium. They had changed each other's chemistry! In that magical moment, in each other's arms, they began to dance.

4. C The night of the shop's grand reopening party, a stage stood outside the shop, lit by hanging lights. The whole community gathered for the big event. Customers sat at outdoor tables, snacking on hot kol nuts. Bernie wanted everything to be perfect. He had even closed the shop for a few days to prepare.

5. D "You caused the leak in the shop?" he said. "I trusted you!" Ember's flames burned with shame. Bernie began to cough. "You will not take over the shop. I no longer retire." He grabbed the lantern and stormed into the shop, with Cinder following close behind.

Chapters 17 & 18

1. A Back inside, as water rose, Ember quickly built a glass cylinder around the Blue Flame. "No, no," she pleaded, hoping the glass would hold. Wade struggled to hold the door in place as windows and pipes began to burst. Water rose faster, covering the family photos on the wall. The lantern that had carried the Blue Flame from Fire Land was swept up in the flow. "Ember, we have to go!" cried Wade. "We have to go now!" "I can't leave!" cried Ember. "I'm sorry to say this," said Wade, "but the shop is done. The Flame is done." "No!" cried Ember. "This is my father's whole life. I'm not going anywhere—"

2. C He took her hand. "Ember, I have no regrets," he said. "You gave me something people search for their whole lives." Ember cried, pleading with him. "But I can't exist in a world without you! I'm sorry I didn't say it before. I love you, Wade." Steam surrounded them. In her sorrow, Ember's most vulnerable light cast rainbows on the wall. Wade instantly felt a sense of peace. "I really do love it when your light does that," he whispered. As they embraced, steam continued to fill the hearth. Silence fell. Wade was gone.

3. B She took a deep breath. It was time to admit what she had come to realize. "I don't want to run the shop. I know that was your dream, but it's not mine. I'm sorry. I'm a bad daughter." She handed the lantern with the Blue Flame to her father.

4. C Wade and Ember began to walk up the ramp of the ship, but Ember turned back. She smiled at Bernie and set down her luggage. Then she knelt on the dock. She stretched her arms out long before her and gave Bernie the Bà Ksô, the Big Bow.

5. D Ember grinned. "I'm sure." Then her expression changed. "Dad, I'm sorry the internship is so far away. I mean, it's the best glass-design company in the world, but who knows if it'll become a real job. And it might not end up being anything—"

엘리멘탈(ELEMENTAL)

1판 1쇄   2024년 1월 2일
1판 3쇄   2024년 8월 19일

지은이   Erin Falligant 롱테일 교육 연구소
편집   강지희 김지혜 홍하늘
디자인   박새롬
마케팅   두잉글 사업본부

기획   김승규
펴낸이   이수영
펴낸곳   롱테일북스
출판등록   제2015-000191호
주소   04033 서울특별시 마포구 양화로 113, 3층(서교동, 순흥빌딩)
홈페이지   www.longtailbooks.co.kr
전자메일   help@ltinc.net

ISBN 979-11-91343-75-5 14740